Casualties of Community Disorder

CRIME & SOCIETY

Casualties of Community Disorder

Women's Careers in Violent Crime

Deborah R. Baskin
and Ira B. Sommers

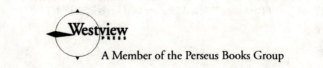

Westview PRESS
A Member of the Perseus Books Group

Crime & Society

Copyright © 1998 by Westview Press, A Member of the Perseus Books Group

Published in 1998 in the United States of America by Westview Press, 5500 Central Avenue, Boulder, Colorado 80301-2877, and in the United Kingdom by Westview Press, 12 Hid's Copse Road, Cumnor Hill, Oxford OX2 9JJ

Library of Congress Cataloging-in-Publication Data
Baskin, Deborah R.
  Casualties of community disorder : women's careers in violent
crime / Deborah R. Baskin, Ira B. Sommers.
    p.   cm. — (Crime & society)
  Includes bibliographical references and index.
  ISBN 0-8133-2993-0 (hc)—ISBN 0-8133-2994-9 (pb)
    1. Female offenders—United States.   2. Violent crimes—United
States.   3. Women—United States—Social conditions.   4. Women—Drug
use—United States.   I. Sommers, Ira Brant.   II. Title.
III. Series: Crime & society (Boulder, Colo.)
HV6791.B37   1998
364.3'74'0973—dc21   97-30633
                                                                          CIP

The paper used in this publication meets the requirements of the American National Standard for Permanence of Paper for Printed Library Materials Z39.48-1984.

PERSEUS
POD
ON DEMAND   10   9   8   7   6   5   4

Alcohol, Drugs, Prostitution, Dealing, Killing—
Each new generation of youth has intensified the consequences of their
unhappiness—
Our schools, parks, and streets are filled with the sights and sounds of rage
and violence—
In my seven years of living in New York I have witnessed the senseless
acts of violence—
On the Brooklyn Bridge I saw three kids (you must be thinking 20-year-
olds, but I mean 9 ½!) cut a man's hand to the bone in an attempt to steal
his mountain bike—
During my few years in public school (K–second grade), I saw three dead
bodies in front of my school—
Also when I walked to school with my parents, I counted crack vials and
did addition by adding different color tops together (e.g., 3 blues + 2
yellows = 5 tops).
These are just three of the harsh realities of inner-city life that I have
witnessed—
I don't fully understand the relaxed use of violence by today's youth—
But there is one thing I'm sure of—if our families, friends, schools, and
communities don't provide supervision, love, respect, and hope for today's
youth, violence will escalate to an even higher level—

—**Arielle Baskin-Sommers**
Age 12

Contents

Tables and Figures

Acknowledgments

This book could not have been written without the countless hours, tears, and hopes that the women we interviewed shared with us. Their wish to have their voices heard so that others may better understand the complexity of their initiation, the desperation that characterized their involvement, and the devastation that came to represent their lives produced the honest and graphic narratives contained within these pages. It is their openness and beneficence for which we forever will be grateful.

We wish to thank, as well, Karen Colvard and the Guggenheim Foundation. Without their initial support, both intellectual and financial, we would not have begun our "journey." Subsequent support from the National Science Foundation (SBR-9207761) and the National Institute of Drug Abuse (5R01DA07374) permitted us to continue our research. The points of view and perspectives expressed in this book do not necessarily reflect the official positions or policies of these grantors.

Our data collection efforts were facilitated by the assistance of Penny Shtull, Tom Sunderland, and Ric Curtis. We appreciate the countless hours they put in and the sensitivity they demonstrated over the years of this project. We are also grateful for their loyalty, especially in light of pressures generated by the "controversial" perspective that emanated from our research. Furthermore, we wish to thank Phil McGuire from the New York Police Department for providing us with the statistical data on arrests for robbery and assault.

We wish to thank several of our friends in particular because of their never-ending interest and critical assessments of our work. Special thanks go to Laurie Meltzer, Lisa Callahan, Gary Silverman, Lois Resnick, Paula Silver, Buffy Miller, and Nancy Jacobs.

There are two people in particular to whom we are deeply indebted. First, we wish to express our thanks to Jeffrey Fagan, our friend and colleague, who sustained, nurtured, and teased us throughout the course of this project. He stood by us and publicly supported us against the oftentimes vitriolic criticisms of others. For this, and his friendship, we are grateful.

Second, we owe our daughter, Arielle Baskin-Sommers, a special thanks. From the age of 3 (she is now 12), Arielle actively participated in this research project. She offered her insights, wisdom, and good humor throughout. Rather than whining about the time we spent on this project, she found ways of being involved. When attending conferences with us, she publicly promoted our work, often speaking authoritatively to other criminologists on the problems of women who are involved in violent street crime. When the flyers for this book first came out, she proudly distributed them and stapled them to every bulletin board near our offices at California State University, Los Angeles. It is to Arielle that this book is dedicated.

Finally, we would like to thank Marcus Boggs, Lisa Wigutoff, Melanie Stafford, and Silvia Hines at Westview Press for their excellent editorial production assistance.

Deborah R. Baskin
Ira B. Sommers

Chapter One

Introduction: Our Journey into the World of Women and Violent Crime

It is August 1989. We are in the midst of our usual summer vacation in which we travel across the Navajo Reservation as it spans the four states of Arizona, Utah, Colorado, and New Mexico. The evening sky appears to be on fire tonight as it displays varying hues of purple, red, and blue. The air is fresh and clear, and the noises are those of coyotes awakening from their daytime naps and of cars whizzing past on highways that cut across the desert.

Back home in Brooklyn, New York, the skies, too, are ablaze. The pollution, humidity, and heat emanating from the concrete city below have turned the sky into a veritable light show, mimicking the desert skies of the West and momentarily distracting the people below from the cacophony of car alarms, heavy traffic, and other street noises. On this evening, a few blocks from our empty apartment, the quiet was shattered by yet another sound.

A 34-year-old woman . . . [was] shot in the face during a robbery . . . a couple of doors from her home. Two . . . women, a 24-year-old and a 26-year-old . . . were arrested and charged with attempted murder, robbery, assault, and criminal possession of a weapon in connection with the shooting and robbery, said police.

She was approached from behind by two women, said police, who shot her, took her wallet containing $320 in cash and fled. . . . The victim's property and two guns—a .380 automatic, which was found on one of the suspects, and a .22 caliber starter's pistol, found nearby— were recovered. (*Park Slope Paper*, 1989)

Apprehension of these women took place under our family room window, in a park that, in the evenings of 1989, was home to a few homeless individuals, a social milieu for the neighborhood alcoholics and wanna-be gang members, as well as a distribution point for a small but busy street-level crack-cocaine market. It was here that these two women were found trying to "cop" some crack with the money that they had just stolen from our neighbor.

Until this event, we had little professional interest in the topic of women and crime. By and large, criminologists concerned with this issue had convinced us that the problem was indeed a small one. They cited available statistics in which female offenders, especially those involved in violent street crime, made up a minuscule and inconsequential proportion of the offender population. Figures provided by these criminologists showed that in any crime category, the female rate of violence never exceeded one-quarter of the male rate and that men were seven times more likely than women to be arrested for a violent crime (Kruttschnitt, 1993). With these data, the majority of criminologists who write about female offending "prove" the insignificance of female involvement (Steffensmeier, 1983; Feinman, 1986; Leonard, 1982; Naffine, 1987; Steffensmeier and Steifel, 1992).

Further, these criminologists developed theories and perspectives that explained away the "offender" label and instead left women who were involved in violent street crime with the dubious distinction of being "victims" (Price and Sokoloff, 1982; Sarri, 1987; Arnold, 1990; Daly, 1992; Chesney-Lind and Shelden, 1992; Lake, 1993). Causal blame for all female involvement in street crime was placed on fathers, brothers, lovers, pimps, and others who "coerced" the women into participation. Thus, if men did not physically and sexually abuse their daughters, forcing them to run away and into a life of crime for survival; if girlfriends and wives were not turned into accomplices, prostitutes, or drug addicts desperate to do anything for a fix or for love; or if these men just did not abandon their families, leaving women with no other options but to commit crime in order to support children, then Donna

Reeds they would all be. That was what these criminologists would have us believe, at least until 1989.

By 1989, the crack-cocaine markets had wreaked havoc on communities already on the brink of decay. News stories reported on the deaths of ordinary citizens, children and adults alike, in the battles over turf, profits, and reputation. Abandoned buildings and lots were overtaken by drug entrepreneurs eager to set up shop. Prostitutes, grandmothers, nieces, and daughters were recruited into various levels of the distribution market. A growing number of children were being born crack-addicted, and the faces of their mothers confronted us on the news every evening.

But when, in 1989, the effects of these drug markets spilled over into our neighborhood, and the histories of these two women offenders was revealed in articles, court reports, and community gossip, the generic explanation of female offending, seemed to us to be inadequate. Further, local newspapers, jumping on the bandwagon to "demonize" women offenders, began to routinely include the gender of the offenders in their crime blotter stories and even ran several feature articles concerning the infiltration of women into the ranks of violent offending.

Community reaction to this event and to subsequent media accounts further piqued our interest in exploring this topic. The neighborhood was buzzing with talk about the new breed of young women offenders. A community group coalesced around the summer night robbery in order to monitor court proceedings. The local sentiment was that these women must be prosecuted and punished to the fullest extent of the law; no plea bargaining, and definitely no sympathy was to be given.

One local fear was that owing to their gender, the actions of these women would be assessed as being less serious than if committed by males and that they would be released to continue preying on our community. A second fear was that of the unknown. If we are now aware of these two women, how many more are there who are lurking behind bushes and trees, in alleyways and stairwells, ready to pounce on us law-abiding citizens?

Our friends, knowing what we did for a living, asked our opinions, and dinner conversation would turn inevitably toward trying to make sense out of the available information. Curious as to whether this particular incident in our neighborhood involving these women robbers was idiosyncratic or whether we were guilty of gender blindness or, worse, of assuming that all violent crimes were committed by men, we undertook this study.

This book represents the culmination of 8 years of investigation that includes interviews with 170 women offenders who were involved in violent street crime and who grew up and were living in New York City during the bulk of their criminal careers. From our work, we found that, as disorganizing social, cultural, and economic influences took hold in vulnerable communities during the 1970s and 1980s, the reigning explanations for violent female offending were cracking under the weight of these changes.

Although some women continue to be forced into violent offending by their significant others or by circumstances related to drug addiction or single parenthood, a growing number of women have found themselves pulled into violent street crime by the same forces that affect their male counterparts. Combinations of individual-level as well as peer, school, and other socializing influences, such as neighborhood changes, have been pulling an increasing number of underclass women in New York City into the ranks of violent offending. In many ways, this book provides a perspective both on the slow and painful demise of the community as a source of support for women who are coming of age today and on the demise of antiquated theories that have permitted us to ignore the changes until now.

Earlier Conceptualizations

To a large extent, prior to the 1990s, studies of female offending focused on criminal activities traditionally associated with the feminine role, such as shoplifting (Cameron, 1964), prostitution and other forms of sexual deviance (Alexander, 1987; Cohen, 1980), and varied but less serious forms of "street deviance" (Carlen, 1988; Miller, 1986). Explanations for these behaviors were marked by stark stereotypical contrasts. Although male criminality was explained in such global terms as the fulfillment of cultural aspirations (Merton, 1957) and peer approval (Sykes and Matza, 1957) or as a result of the failure to establish stakes in conformity (Hirschi, 1969) or in favorable definitions of the law (Sutherland, 1939), explanations for women rarely strayed far from home. Female criminality was attributed mostly to biological (Lombroso and Ferrero, 1895; Pollak, 1950) or psychological (Freud, 1933) factors or confined to home or family influences (Morris, 1964).

When explanations were tied to changes in the world outside of the individual or home, they were linked to the movement for women's liberation. Several works, beginning with Adler's *Sisters in Crime* (1975) and Simon's *Women and Crime* (1975), linked the contemporary women's movement to the increasing involvement of women in criminal activity (see also Noblit and Burcart, 1976; Deming, 1977; Adler and Simon, 1979; Adler, 1981; Austin, 1982). Their argument has been that women's liberation not only increased social and legal equality but also enhanced women's opportunities for criminal involvement. Thus, at the same time that women were making gains in the world of legitimate enterprise, they were also making headway in a wide variety of criminal activities, ranging from property offenses to terrorism (Klemesrud, 1978). These advances were attributed to changes in female personality (i.e., increased competitiveness, instrumentalism), structural opportunities (i.e., new employment settings), and behaviors (i.e., greater willingness and ability to assume male roles and responsibilities; Adler, 1975; Simon, 1975). However, as we shall see from the women in our study, the outcome of these transformations contradicted the success story expected by proponents of this perspective.

Whereas the liberation thesis attempted to formulate gender-specific explanations for the escalating involvement of women in criminal activity, there are those who argued that traditional (male) theories of criminality, with or without some minor modification, could explain the crime patterns of women. Smith and Paternoster (1987:142) identified several studies that attempted to test the applicability of such traditional perspectives as *social bonding* (Jensen and Raymond, 1976; Elliott and Voss, 1974; Smith, 1979; Krohn and Massey, 1980), *differential opportunity* (Datesman, Scarpitti, and Stephenson, 1975; Smith, 1979; Rankin, 1980; Simons, Miller, and Aigner, 1980), *deterrence theory* (Burkett and Jensen, 1975; Anderson, Chiricos, and Waldo, 1977; Smith, 1979), and *differential association* (Elliott and Voss, 1974; Simons, Miller, and Aigner, 1980) to female criminality.

The generalizability thesis suffers from key problems, however. All of the studies noted previously focused only on youth who were engaged in relatively minor delinquency, such as marijuana use or status offenses. Moreover, even in the best of these studies, the evidence has been limited and inconclusive. Further, the failure to situate analyses within "bounded spheres of interaction" (Sullivan, 1989:9), that is, specific communities in which choices concerning crime, work, and family are made, contributes to the sterility of this perspective. Perhaps more important, as a result of these weaknesses this thesis cannot represent women's lives and social worlds, and by extension, it fails to explain women's criminality.

Even when attempts have been made to explore women's worlds, serious questions remain. Some have argued that the increasing feminization of poverty forces women into a wider array of criminal activities, including violent street crime. For instance, Steven Box, in his review of research on unemployment and crime, found that "the most plausible reason for [the increase in women's participation in conventional criminality] is that more women have become economically marginalized" (1987:43). Nonetheless, in its attempt to link the feminization of poverty to increased participation of women in conventional criminality, this perspective fails to account for the fact that most poor women are, in fact, law-abiding.

In addition, because of its overly economistic view of human behavior, this perspective cannot answer the fundamental question: Why now? Without exploring the social, cultural, and political transformations that have affected underclass communities, this perspective cannot delineate the link between poverty and criminality. As a result, this explanation, for many of the same reasons as the generalization thesis, leaves that connection unclear and in need of further investigation.

One of the earliest analyses of the connection between poverty and criminality was done by Pat Carlen, a British sociologist who traced the criminal careers of 39 women offenders through life history interviews (Carlen, 1988). With Carlen's help, these women were able to identify four factors, in various combinations, that constituted the bases for their involvement in criminal careers. Poverty, placement in residential homes outside of the family of origin during childhood (e.g., juvenile correctional facilities), drug and alcohol addiction, and the quest for excitement all were related to the development of their criminal careers. As a result of the difficulties engendered by these conditions, the women in Carlen's study were cut off from developing commitments to both traditional family ties (the "gender deal") and legitimate employment opportunities (the "class deal"). Instead, they embarked on long careers in crime that were punctuated with stays in correctional facilities. These periods of incarceration dashed any hopes of desistance by further narrowing the options available to them upon release.

Despite its improvement over earlier and even contemporaneous works in this area, Carlen's analysis of women, crime, and poverty falls short in answering what were, to us, two fundamental questions: How are women's criminal careers (e.g., initiation, persistence, and termination) circumscribed specifically by *gender*? And what accounts for the increasing pull of certain groups of women into the world of violent crime? Although it is clear that specific subgroups of males contribute disproportionately to the violent crime problem, how can we account for the wide variation in violent crime participation when race and age variables are included in the equation?

Overview of the Book

This book has three interrelated directions. First, we examine how processes of urban structural and economic decay have combined to create new and invigorate old criminogenic factors. We identify factors that cut across gender categories (e.g., peers, general drug abuse, victimization, criminal opportunities) and others that apply primarily to women (e.g., decline in family and neighborhood supervision, earlier termination of education, and crack addiction). These factors have resulted in alarming changes in women's participation in violent street crime. Second, we explore how personal decisions related to such participation are mediated by women's experiences and understanding of their present environment. Third, we describe a framework we have developed for understanding how the *interaction* between personal history, social processes, and a changing inner city structures women's participation in violent crime. More specifically, early socialization experiences (child abuse and neglect; family, peer, and community networks), substance abuse and criminal careers, and the movement in and out of conventional activities (education, legitimate employment, marriage) are linked to broader social, economic, and situational processes.

The Research Enterprise

In order to explore these issues, we consulted a wide range of sources. We collected official data on arrests, incarcerations, and neighborhood socioeconomic indicators. Although we are aware of the limitations inherent in using official data (see Bursik and Grasmick, 1993), the purpose here was not to use them as direct indicators of the phenomena under study, but rather to answer some general questions: Have there been changes in the trends and patterns of women's participation in violent street crime and in the communities in which they live? Furthermore, these sorts of data paint broad brushstrokes so that finer, more richly detailed data can be contextualized.

So that we might add substance to the study as well as obtain more direct indicators, we conducted in-depth, life history interviews with 170 women who had committed violent felony crimes (robbery, assault, homicide) in New York City. We chose the life history technique for several reasons. For one, we were dissatisfied with the current hegemony of two competing explanations for violent crime: that of rational choice and that of no choice. Clearly, it would be easier to say, as do many politicians and a growing number of criminologists, that these women, plain and simple, *choose* to become violent offenders. It is equally easy to say, as do many social scientists, that these women have *no* choice but to become involved in crime. However, it may be that the more accurate understanding is somewhere in between these two points—somewhere in the terrain made up by the social worlds through which these women pass.

Our interest in examining the pushes and pulls of the various social worlds encountered and experienced by these women was facilitated by the life history technique. Through these interviews, the women were able to represent to us a level of activity, creativity, and human agency that might otherwise not have been attainable. It permitted us to understand how their experiences, relationships, and other processes structurally and experientially established how the "choices" they faced emerged and how they were then defined. In this way, we were better able to understand how embedded their criminal careers were within larger social worlds that, by and large, reinforced their involvement.

The value of life history interviews in this process lies in the wealth of data that is collected as well as the usefulness of the interviews in facilitating the development of "thick descriptions" (Geertz, 1973). With the assistance of highly trained interviewers, 170 women developed autobiographical accounts of their life experiences that have enabled us to appreciate better the wide range of everyday processes that contributed to the establishment and maintenance of their criminal careers.

Furthermore, these types of interviews allowed us to assess the viability of existing theories for explaining the pathways and careers of the women in this study. And it was interesting to find that women rejected the explanation of being "forced" into crime with the notably common comment that they "would never go up the river for some man." At the same time, they rejected the suggestions of the politicians and rational choice advocates that they made "choices." Again, for them, it was somewhere in between. Since people live their lives according to their own interpretations of their circumstances, the views of reality that these women provide give us a more extensive understanding of the social worlds of violent street crime.

To tap into these overlapping social worlds, we interviewed the women around certain general focal areas, including the women's perceptions of family, peer, and neighborhood relationships and characteristics; school and employment background; official and self-reported involvement in crime; victimization histories (personal victimization, own perpetration of abuse, and witnessing of others' abuse); alcohol and drug use; as well as treatment, residential, and custodial experiences. Through conversations with these women around these issues, we hoped to construct a context in which salient life events could be thickly described.

However, our intent in this endeavor was not to reduce their lives and an explanation of their offending to these focal areas. Neither were we motivated to provide a "scientific" account of the relationships between these focal points and the involvement in violent street crime. Instead, we were trying to formulate a description of how these women imagine their lives, a description that they, themselves, would be able to recognize when we retold their stories. Therefore, our ability to bring the reader in touch with the lives of these women took on great importance.

Surely one could raise issues concerning the reliability and validity of the recounting of these life experiences. However, several factors suggest that the women represented to us their lives as they perceived them. First, there was little reason for these women to deceive us. We made it clear to all of the women not only that we were unaffiliated with any agency involved in their lives but that even under the most serious threats, we would not divulge any information. Further, we destroyed any materials that might link the women with specific responses, and we coded other materials so that they could not be identified with any particular person. We spent a considerable amount of time with each respondent reviewing these assurances, so that by the time we got into the interview, they appeared quite comfortable.

Whether the women *accurately* recalled life events was not much of an issue for us, either. We were far more concerned with the accounts the women used to describe their lives. We wanted to know what *they* considered to be the salient life events that led them to who they were now. Therefore, we took the women back to early childhood experiences, rooted the conversations in discussions of where they were living and what grade they were in, and worked with them to establish a time line that was punctuated by their identification of key life events.

Certainly, the accounts of their lives were full of contradictions. It was easy enough to clear up temporal issues, but for the most part we appreciated and included the contradictions. Like everyone's life, the lives of these women are made up of contradictions, and to try and smooth them out by forcing the women to give a linear description would have truly threatened the believability of their stories. Further, by retaining the seemingly contradictory elements of their stories, we were able to better appreciate the "thickness" of the descriptions they were offering.

Nonetheless, in our acts of conversing, recording, and analyzing, we have necessarily imposed a coherence on their statements that permits "outsiders," such as ourselves and our readers, to have better access to understanding the lives of these women. We believe as does Geertz that such an imposition "is not as fatal as it sounds, for in fact . . . it is not necessary to know everything in order to understand something" (1973:20). And despite its inconclusiveness, we would like to understand how, given general and gendered mainstream proscriptions, these women became and remained involved in violent street crime.

The Sample

We found women who were willing to engage in these lengthy, in-depth, intimate conversations by tapping into several sources. We consulted arrest and arraignment logs, state corrections databases, and the files of other researchers who had access to women who, at the time of the project, were actively involved in violent criminal offending. The latter group was recruited through arrangements with fieldworkers engaged in ethnographic research in Central Harlem and Washington Heights, in Manhattan, and Bushwick, in Brooklyn, between September 1992 and August 1994. The long-term relationships of these fieldworkers to women who were involved in a wide array of street activities, from drug distribution and use to nondrug criminality, provided us with fairly easy access to participants known to engage in street violence. From this setting, we were able to interview 85 women.

The sample of women arraigned on violent felony charges was obtained by checking arraignment calendars for the time period between January and June 1990. Access to complete court records permitted us to weed out women whose arrests were related directly to domestic violence. Official data were collected on 176 women, and letters inviting them to participate in this study were sent to all for whom there was a recent address. Out of this group, we completed interviews with 43 women.

In addition to the community-based samples, New York State Department of Correctional Services databases were examined in order to draw a similar incarcerated sample. Women committed to Bedford Hills and Bayview Correctional Facilities for a felony offense (murder/manslaughter, assault, robbery, weapons possession/use, burglary, arson, kidnapping) during 1990 were eligible to participate in our study. Women whose violent acts were of a domestic nature were, again, excluded. Official records data were collected on 93 women who fit study criteria. Of these, 42 women agreed to complete interviews.

It is interesting to note that each of the women we interviewed came from one of the seven hyperghettoized New York City neighborhoods identified in the *New York Times* (1993) as producing 75 percent of the state's entire prison population. The vast majority of the women in our study came from three neighborhoods in particular: Central Harlem and Washington Heights in Manhattan, and Bushwick in Brooklyn. The clustering of these women primarily into three neighborhoods permitted us to explore the situational dynamics, motivations, and personal contexts that mediated their decisions to participate in crime within a small number of community contexts that shared strikingly similar structural, cultural, and political processes. In this way, we were able to examine the concentration effects of poverty on criminality within a population that was fairly homogeneous in terms of some of the more global background factors. And it was from the interviews that we were able to pick up some of the nuances and distinctions that characterized their individual biographies.

Early Criticism

But we are getting ahead of ourselves. The road between our initial curiosity concerning the two women in our neighborhood and the full-blown investigation we ultimately undertook was, mildly put, rocky. Almost from the start, a few vocal criminologists and community program advocates began to rail against our questions as being too controversial, even dangerous. They claimed that we ignored the *real* numbers and patterns of women's involvement in violent street crime and that our sensationalism of this issue was going to lead, directly, to the overuse of incarceration for women offenders.

Although our main interest was not in the "objective" reality of female involvement in violent street crime, we did choose to respond to our critics. Further, we thought that by examining the available, official data, we might put the action of the two women in our neighborhood into some broader perspective. Therefore, we turned our attention to assessing the violent crime trends and patterns in New York City.

Given our interest in exploring whether the violent offenses committed by the two women in our neighborhood were aberrations or indicative of any larger patterns, and in order to respond to our increasingly vociferous critics, we obtained New York City arrest data for 1980–1994. We were interested to find that when crime rates were disaggregated by race, gender, and age, more complex patterns of criminal involvement were revealed. Being "male" or being "female" turned out not to accurately predict involvement in violent street crime. Hidden behind these gross categories are subtler influences that provide a clearer picture of the violent crime problem.

Subsequent Chapters

In Chapter 2, we present the specific findings from this analysis and offer a social structural explanation for the observed patterns. This explanation roots the violent crime problem squarely within the everyday life experiences of women growing up in underclass communities. Regardless of race, age, or gender, people from underclass communities are involved disproportionately in violent street crime.

But how does residence in areas characterized by high concentrations of poverty influence *women's* decisions to participate in violent street crime? In Chapter 3, we present the women's descriptions of how living in communities distinguished by their intensified economic and social dislocation; growing drug markets; demographic changes; and situational factors related to family, school, and peer relations contributed to their participation in violent street crime.

In this chapter, we also examine how changes in the strength and composition of family networks and relations and the decline in prosocial role models and community institutions combine to "liberate" these women from the traditional gender-based constraints on involvement in violent street crime. Furthermore, we assess the effects of changes in local drug markets on the underground economy. With the introduction of crack-cocaine markets into underclass neighborhoods, new and phenomenally different opportunity structures were created. The social and economic norms associated with these markets combined with other elements to institutionalize violence as a way of negotiating survival on this terrain.

Furthermore, in this chapter, we examine the processes of entry and initiation into violent street crime. Here, we focus on the complex pushes and pulls that impact on women's lives at several stages preceding their criminal involvement. We take into account the salience and sequencing of various factors and how they may vary with age of initiation.

In many ways, this chapter offers the strongest challenge to the traditional perspective on violent female offending. Although we do not discount the role that victimization and drug abuse play in the careers of some women engaged in street violence, the women we interviewed offered different perspectives on how direct a role, if any, these factors played in terms of their own *initiation* into violent crime. These perspectives were frequently at variance with the more traditional explanations.

Many of the women we interviewed reported that their initiation into violent street offending was due to many of the same sets of factors that accounted for the initiation of their male counterparts (e.g., peers, search for excitement and adventure, opportunity structures, and neighborhood effects). Weak attachments to prosocial institutions, lack of positive parental supervision, associations with deviant peers, and other social and economic processes prevalent in severely distressed communities lay the groundwork for increased female involvement in violent street crime. The women we spoke with described, in great detail, the role that these neighborhood effects played in their initiation.

Nonetheless, at least initially, the majority of the women we interviewed attempted to become involved in the legal job market. At the same time, however, making money remained tied to their concern with "living large." Concerns over these two spheres of activity influenced the women as they walked across the terrains of the workaday world, family relationships, friendships, neighborhood, and other social arrangements. In addition, these concerns helped to define their cultural lives: how the women spent time, forms of self-expression and identity, public and private moments, and the use of drugs and drinking. Ultimately, the deviant street network took increasing prominence in the women's quest for self-identity and expression.

One cannot underestimate the role that neighborhood effects and the networks they generated played in the lives of the women we interviewed. Individuals are members of distinct communities that mediate between them and the larger society. It was within their local communities that these women engaged in social interaction and made decisions regarding school, work, and family. And it was within these local communities that they devised ways of coping with the demands imposed on them by the larger social structure. Community levels of dysfunction and economic and social dislocation, as well as the presence of a well-developed illegitimate opportunity structure, shaped the lifestyles and routine activities engaged in by these women.

In Chapter 5, we examine the actual decision-making processes used by these women in planning and carrying out the illegal behaviors in which they were involved. We spoke with them about their motivations, various situational impediments (e.g., intoxication), and choices of locations, weapons, victims, and accomplices. We present the accounts the women provided themselves to describe and justify the dynamics of violent crime involvement.

Drug use and distribution play a critical role in the continuing involvement of these women in their violent crime careers. We explore the use of violence in the context of drug dealing, the pharmacological effects of certain drugs on participation in violent street crime, and the extent to which the women were victimized by virtue of being sellers or users.

Further, we explore the situational contexts surrounding two major violent street crimes: robbery and assault. We see how routine activities and lifestyles interact with aspects of the communities in which these women live. We look at how community levels of family dysfunction and economic and social dislocation, as well as the presence of illegitimate opportunity structures, affect these women's participation in robbery and assault.

Despite the fact that these women's lives were filled with crime, drugs, and violence, there were some who eventually exited from their criminal and drug careers. In Chapter 6, we describe the social processes and turning points that triggered these women's departure from street deviance. We conclude the chapter with the presentation of a three-stage model for understanding desistance from violent crime.

In the conclusion, we deconstruct the concept of female offender in order to better appreciate the complexity of women's involvement in criminal and drug careers. Further, we emphasize the importance of the developmental perspective in the timing and sequence of initiation into delinquency and crime and of desistance. Finally, we assess contemporary policies regarding violence, especially in terms of gender.

Chapter Two

Crime and Urban Distress: Patterns of Violent Offending

When we first saw the movie *New Jack City,* we were startled by how nonchalantly the character Keisha (Vanessa Williams) shot her victims at close range, point blank, with a bullet to the head. Did women like her really exist outside the confines of a screenwriter's imagination? Were the actions of the two women in our neighborhood anomalies? Or were we blind to the possibility of women being involved in violent street crime, therefore assuming that all offenders were males? Our curiosity piqued, we began to take note of gender when we read newspaper stories or heard crime reports on the nightly news. We noticed with interest news stories in which women were reported to be the principal offenders in violent street events. For instance, a 1990 news story reported the following:

> Carjacking sent Carla to Rikers Island. But, she joked, that's not the only crime she committed—just the only one she got caught for. She's lost track of the number of robberies she's participated in.
>
> "My little sister, she's 11, she just wrote to me," Carla said. Her face lit up with a grin of big-sisterly pride. "She said she wants to be just like me." (*New York Times*, 1990)

Similarly in a 1990 news story:

Eleven young girls from a Manhattan neighborhood were arrested for attacking, robbing and beating people in a chain of incidents spanning a period of several months. (Peters, 1993)

A more recent story in the *New York Times* stated the following:

At first glance, the series of robberies at a Brooklyn housing project had the trappings of typical holdups. The robbers, wearing hats and masks, followed victims into elevators and stairways, put a gun to their heads and dashed away with money and/or jewelry. One thing, however, was noticeably different. The suspects were women. Rhonda, 26, and Cheri, 23, were eventually arrested and charged with 10 counts of robbery, assault and possession of weapons.

One victim recalled:

I went into the elevator, the tall woman held the door for me. I pressed the button for the 13th floor. They had their backs to me. I could smell alcohol on their breath. One had a bottle of Wild Irish Rose in her pocket. When the elevator got close to my floor, the tall one pulled out a gun and said, "Don't move. Don't yell. Just give us your jewelry." One girl pulled my ring and when it didn't come off fast enough the tall one hit me with the gun. She hit me twice in the head. Blood was squirting out of my eye. (*New York Times*, 1995)

Reports of female street violence were not just New York stories or events that occurred only in big cities.
In 1992, *Newsweek* covered the following story:

Tragedy came to Crosby, Texas, over breakfast in the high school cafeteria. The victim was Arthur Jack, 17, captain of the varsity football team. According to witnesses, Jack was helping himself to orange juice in the serving line when he heard someone say, "You called me a bitch." He looked up to see another student, identified by police as LaKeeta Cadoree, 15, pointing a .38-caliber revolver. Jack tried to take cover but the shooter was too quick: hit in the back by a bullet that traveled upward to pierce his heart, he died on the floor behind the serving counter. (*Newsweek*, 1992)

In a *Los Angeles Times* report on female offenders, Tamara, 14, describes the casual use of violence:

My friends, they won't let me get my hands on a gun. They say I'm trigger happy. One time I had a gun, I saw one of my enemies and that made me boil over. I would see her and think, "Oh man, she just says stupid things. She's like a little rat." I go, "Hey, I have to put a stop to this." I was like really seriously about to shoot her. My friends, they were like, "It's not worth 25 to life." I'm like, "Hey, it's my life. I serve 25 years, I'm still 39 when I get out." My friends, they talked me out of it. Then later I thought, if I had done her, she wouldn't be here to bother me. (*Los Angeles Times*, 1996)

Although we did notice an increasing number of news stories in which women were portrayed as actively involved in violent street crime, we were not yet convinced that these reports were any more than the *demonizing* or sensationalizing of which we spoke earlier. As a result, we decided to turn to police data in order to get a better idea of some of the trends and patterns of women's involvement in violent street crime. We obtained arrest counts by crime type for the years 1980–1994 in New York City. To adjust for potential year-to-year variations in reporting and recording practices, these data were aggregated and analyzed in 5-year time blocks.

First we looked at trends. We were interested in whether, in fact, there was an increase in women's involvement in violent street crime. As you can see, the data from Table 2.1 indeed indicate a dramatic growth in female involvement in violent crime. Female arrests for robbery and aggravated assault increased 77.5 percent and 56 percent, respectively, between 1980 and 1984 and between 1990 and 1994. Furthermore, the *proportion* of violent crimes committed by women over this time period also increased for the crimes of robbery and aggravated assault, although not for homicide. Thus, the characterizations of women's increased involvement in violent street crime were not fabrications of either the movie or news industry.

However, comparable data for males also indicate increases. For robbery there was a 23 percent increase in arrests, and for assault, a 31 percent rise in arrests. In terms of absolute numbers, men continued to commit much more violent street crime than women. Over the 15-year time period (1980–1994), males were approximately 14 times more likely to be arrested for murder/manslaughter. The ratios for robbery (11:1) and aggravated assault (6:1) indicate that females were much less frequently involved in violent offending than males. The finding that gender produces a striking

TABLE 2.1   Violent Crime Arrests, New York City, 1980–1994

	1980–1984		1985–1989		1990–1994	
Crime Type	M	F	M	F	M	F
Homicide	5,630	468	5,820	436	6,290	347
Robbery	97,847	6,718	110,849	10,171	120,765	11,923
Assault	72,790	10,960	101,712	17,213	95,649	17,129

difference in the extent and nature of interpersonal violence does not come as a surprise. Men *do* dominate official reports of violent crime. And regardless of data source, they appear to engage disproportionately in the most harmful acts of violence (Kruttschnitt, 1993). However, as you will soon see, looking at crime figures only in gross generalizations of male and female can obscure some serious and important information.

Sex, Race, Age, and Violent Offending

In accepting a simple male-female dichotomy, recent research has done little to challenge or understand the "gender ratio problem" (Daly and Chesney-Lind, 1987). Prior analyses of violent offending generally have not considered variations across subgroups based on age, race, and sex. Neither have they considered the possible effects that situational or community-level factors might have on an individual's experiences with violence.

To address this issue, we again used New York City arrest data to examine rates of offending for specific sex-race-age groups. The data on arrests for murder/manslaughter, robbery, and aggravated assault were aggregated from raw data made available by the New York City Police Department in the form of arrest counts by crime type, race and age subgroups, and year (1987–1992). In conjunction with population estimates from the census data (1987 and 1990), we computed sex-race-age- and crime-specific arrest rates that take into account sex distributions in the population. A 6-year average rate was computed to stabilize random fluctuations, a practice followed in previous research (Messner, 1983; Sampson, 1985; Allan and Steffensmeier, 1989).

Table 2.2 presents violent crime arrest *rates* for males and females from 1987 to 1992. Again, when you look only at male-female dif-

TABLE 2.2   Violent Crime Arrest Rates per 100,000 for Males and Females, New York City, 1987–1992

Crime Type	Males	Females
Homicide	155.39	8.47
Robbery	3,052.49	249.60
Aggravated assault	2,586.06	391.83

Note. The target category for the estimated rates of offending includes blacks, Hispanics, and whites. Other races are excluded. Data sources include the New York City Police Department and U.S. Bureau of Census, Current Population Reports.

ferences, you continue to find glaring disparities. Males are 18 times more likely to be arrested for homicide than are females; 12 times more likely for robbery; and 7 times more likely for aggravated assault.

When arrest rates for violent crimes are classified by race and sex, however, a number of interesting and important patterns emerge (Table 2.3). For instance, despite the fact that black and Hispanic men still have significantly higher rates of offending than all other groups, black *women* are more likely to be arrested for robbery and aggravated assault than are white *males*.

Again, simple male-female dichotomies obscure real differences not only between groups but within groups. Consider the patterns that exist within gender. Black females have higher arrest rates across all of the crime categories than either white or Hispanic females, and Hispanic females have higher arrest rates than their white counterparts. Yet Hispanic females also have offending rates much more similar to white males than to any other group (Table 2.4). White females have the lowest offending rates of all subgroups, across all categories.

Let's break these groups down again, this time by age. Previous research has produced contradictory findings regarding age-specific rates of offending. Some studies have suggested that the peak ages of violent activity vary little by sex (Hindelang, 1981; Kruttschnitt, 1993). Others indicate that violent female criminal careers both begin and peak earlier than those of males (Weiner and Wolfgang, 1989). In addition to these divergent findings, it is problematic that previous studies have tended to examine age-sex patterns without regard to race (Chilton and Datesman, 1987).

TABLE 2.3   Violent Crime Arrest Rates per 100,000 (and Female Percentage of
Arrests) by Sex and Race of Offender, New York City, 1987–1992

Type of Offender	Homicide	Robbery	Assault
White males	26.12	473.95	804.75
Black males	347.79	7,757.82	5,363.26
Hispanic males	192.94	2,939.49	2,978.03
White females	1.54	43.10	71.34
Black females	20.30	648.10	1,002.65
Hispanic females	8.10	189.04	306.02

Note. Data sources include the New York City Police Department and U.S. Bureau of Census, Current Population Reports.

TABLE 2.4   Ratios of the Estimated Rates of Offending per 100,000 by Offenders'
Sex and Race, New York City, 1987–1992

Type of Offender	Homicide	Robbery	Assault
BM/HF	42.94	41.04	17.53
WM/HF	3.22	2.51	2.33
HM/HF	23.82	15.55	9.73
BM/WF	225.84	180.00	75.18
HM/WF	125.29	68.20	41.74
WM/WF	16.96	11.00	11.28
BM/BF	17.13	11.97	5.35
HM/BF	9.50	4.54	2.97
WM/BF	1.29	.73	.80
BF/WF	13.18	15.04	14.05
BF/HF	2.51	3.43	3.28
HF/WF	5.26	4.39	4.29
BM/HM	1.80	2.64	1.80
BM/WM	13.32	16.37	6.66
HM/WM	7.39	6.20	3.70

BM=black male; WM=white male; HM=Hispanic male; BF=black female;
WF=white female; HF=Hispanic female

In Table 2.5, we include race in our analysis. The race-age offending rates for males exhibit a pattern of initial incline over the teenage years followed by a decline after the young adult years. In the case of murder, robbery, and assault, the arrest rates for males, regardless of race, are highest for the mid teens to the mid twenties.

TABLE 2.5   Violent Crime Arrest Rates per 100,000 by Sex, Race, and Age of
Offender, New York City, 1987–1992

Type of Offender	Homicide	Robbery	Assault
White males			
<15	2.76	162.13	147.93
15–19	86.24	1,538.76	2,359.50
20–24	66.23	1,339.33	2,021.26
25–29	44.01	1,066.38	1,519.48
30–39	34.39	684.94	1,269.98
40+	11.38	61.92	271.52
Black males			
<15	49.67	3,666.39	1,022.35
15–19	1,078.07	22,559.36	10,243.85
20–24	1,061.11	20,963.89	12,779.17
25–29	635.82	15,180.60	12,280.60
30–39	305.06	6,367.61	8,091.69
40+	86.19	654.41	2,307.14
Hispanic males			
<15	26.47	1,170.02	445.56
15–19	564.44	9,610.00	6,008.89
20–24	462.32	7,146.87	6,759.90
25–29	350.88	4,840.76	5,946.02
30–39	219.18	2,282.03	4,401.29
40+	64.58	343.59	1,533.30
White females			
<15	2.06	20.97	15.63
15–19	1.97	125.37	158.93
20–24	1.52	130.50	178.30
25–29	1.39	128.83	165.04
30–39	2.69	64.13	149.78
40+	1.06	5.91	23.64
Black females			
<15	1.66	596.44	298.43
15–19	40.44	1,485.34	1,771.49
20–24	57.73	1,523.97	2,332.24
25–29	42.19	1,347.78	2,410.49
30–39	34.62	608.33	1,576.92
40+	5.53	48.89	301.22
Hispanic females			
<15	.77	90.94	77.84
15–19	10.85	469.63	566.16
20–24	17.00	504.78	615.30
25–29	19.93	351.05	568.11
30–39	13.40	189.00	513.40
40+	4.15	20.36	123.30

By contrast, violent female offending peaks at a later age for robbery than it does for males (20–24 compared to 15–19). The female age distribution for assault is similar to the male distribution, highest in the early twenties. There is one notable exception. The peak age for assault for white males is 15–19.

In the case of homicide, we found that female involvement continues at a relatively equal rate into the 30s, whereas the male rate drops off in the 30s. This continued level of involvement may be due to the greater tendency for women who kill to do so within a domestic arrangement, such as against a spouse or significant other (Mann, 1988; Wolfgang and Ferracuti, 1975).

Overall, these findings suggest that looking at sex and age differences in terms of violent offending without also considering the effects of race will produce incomplete and potentially misleading interpretations. For instance, the data in Table 2.5 show that black females under the age of 15 are substantially more likely to be involved in robbery than white males their own age (596 compared to 162). Further, the robbery offending rates between these two subgroups remain fairly consistent across the other age categories. And we see the same pattern for assault.

The continued tendency to disregard the interactive effects of gender, race, and age (and class) in studies of patterns of female offending is unfortunate. As you can see from our examination, the need to move beyond the gross categories of male and female is imperative. Disparities in the trends and patterns of violent offending between black women and their white and Hispanic counterparts, as well as the comparisons with white males, would have been impossible to discern without the foregoing analysis. However, now that we have this disturbing information, we can no longer ignore the fact that the gender-ratio relationship is spurious. Neither can we leave this issue to rest. We must ask these questions: Why do black females exhibit such relatively high rates of violence? What accounts for the increase in female violent offending, particularly for blacks and Hispanics, over the past decade?

Making Sense of Race and Violent Street Crime

In terms of understanding the participation of black women in violent street crime, a number of explanations have been suggested.

Mostly, they emerge from a gender-neutral perspective in which culture, structure, or some other variable cuts across all socio-demographic categories. Perhaps the most prominent among these theories is that of the subculture of violence.

Rooted in earlier work by Wolfgang and Ferracuti (1975), some criminologists have attempted to explain variations in crime rates among different groups in our society (Northerners vs. Southerners, Easterners vs. Westerners, blacks vs. whites, males vs. females) by arguing that the "more criminal" group possesses a set of values that is not only conducive to violence but actually promotes its use under prescribed circumstances. In terms of racial differences, the argument, simply put, is that since life in urban black ghettos is perceived as tough and fatalistic, aggressiveness, in the form of violence, is not only necessary but valued as a means of surviving and enhancing one's self-image. People who do not follow the norms are criticized or ridiculed by others in the subcultural group.

As appealing an explanation as the subculture of violence thesis may sound—and there have been many times that we have either used it or heard it being used to explain the "undesirable" behaviors of *other* groups of people—the evidence to support it has been, at best, equivocal (Ball-Rokeach, 1973; Erlanger, 1974; Hartnagel, 1980; Kornhauser, 1978; Loftin and Hill, 1974; Parker, 1989; Sampson, 1987; Williams and Flewelling, 1987; Williams 1984). Yet, perhaps in part owing to its ability to separate *us* good people from those *other* bad people, various forms of subcultural theories continue to hold the attention of scholars and policymakers, especially when concerning the issue of crime in the black community (Lane, 1986; Katz, 1988). Whether employed by those conservatives who see crime as rooted in the constitution of black people (Wilson and Hernstein, 1985) or by the liberals who view the rise of a black subculture of violence as initially emerging out of a historical process of marginalization (Wolfgang and Ferracuti, 1975; Curtis, 1975), this thesis continues, to this day, to be tremendously persuasive.

Nonetheless, this perspective has been vigorously challenged by those who argue that *structure,* not *culture,* is more important in understanding street violence. For instance, Robert Sampson (1985) looks to broader structural forces in terms of the impact that they have on other social and cultural institutions, specifically the family. Therefore, instead of focusing on the *values* that allegedly differentiate the urban black family from other subgroups, the broader *structures* of increasing black male joblessness and decreasing opportunities for marriage become the differentiating factors.

This perspective does not devalue the role played by the family in socializing its young. But it does view the ability of the family to positively socialize its children as mediated by larger, *structural* forces of socioeconomic and political resources. Therefore, the more separated the family is from the resources that allow one to be part of a larger network of relatives, friends, and other social institutions, the more difficult it is to perform necessary socialization and supervisory functions.

This still does not explain why *black women's* violent offending rates are so severe and why those of *Hispanic women* are showing an upward turn, and unfortunately, we could not find a satisfactory explanation in the existing criminological literature. However, we did come across a very forceful and systematic treatment of the links among politics, economics, culture, and individual behaviors in the work of William Julius Wilson (1987, 1991). Although he does not deal specifically with the issue of criminal involvement, he argues that the growing geographic concentration of urban poverty[1] and the social isolation accompanying it have produced serious and extremely negative consequences in certain segments of our urban environments.

Wilson has stated that living in extremely impoverished neighborhoods where access to jobs and job networks, quality schools, and conventional role models is severely compromised has the concentrated and highly deleterious effect of diminishing the strength of formal and informal social control, limiting academic success and aspirations, isolating from economic networks, and distorting social perceptions. The appeal of this perspective is that it does not dichotomize *culture* and *structure*. It shows, instead, how the urban transformations of the last decades impact both the structure of opportunities and the social perceptions of this structure. Thus, it is not sufficient to recognize the importance of macrostructural constraints; it is imperative to understand the cultural significance of life in extreme poverty.

It is our belief that the effects of the social and institutional transformation of the inner city are important for understanding the disproportionate involvement of black females (and males) in violent crime. A social context that includes poor schools, a lack of legitimate job opportunities, inadequate job information networks, and weak community organizations not only gives rise to weak labor-force attachment (Wilson, 1991), but also increases the probability that individuals will be constrained to seek income derived from illegal or deviant activities. Consequently, violence and drug involvement may be seen as adaptive strategies to cope with extreme social and economic deprivation and the adverse reactions of individuals to perceptions of their deprivation and isolation from conventional economic opportunities.

Why such an impact on black people? Recent studies show that the proportion of the poor who live in ghettos varies dramatically by race (Jargowsky and Bane, 1990; Massey and Eggers, 1990; Tobier, 1984). Of the 2.4 million ghetto poor in the United States, 65 percent are black, 22 percent are Hispanic, and 13 percent are non-Hispanic and other races (Jargowsky and Bane, 1990). Therefore, one would expect that women living in extreme poverty (i.e., neighborhoods with high concentrations of poverty) would be involved disproportionately in criminal activities and that black women would be more likely to reside in these neighborhoods.

In an attempt to examine these propositions empirically, we analyzed the official arrest histories by place of residence for 341 women arrested in two New York City boroughs (Manhattan and Brooklyn) for violent felonies. In order to measure concentration of poverty, we assigned every offender a 1990 census tract code based on their address at the time of their instant offense.[2] Census tracts were classified in terms of the percentage of families living below the poverty threshold. Places with *low* concentrations of poverty are tracts where less than 20 percent of the families have incomes below the poverty threshold; *moderate* concentrations of poverty are tracts where 20–30 percent of the families have incomes below the poverty threshold; and *high* concentrations of poverty are tracts where more than 30 percent of the families have incomes below the poverty threshold.

Our findings indicate that the concentration of poverty is associated positively with the level of criminal activity. The average numbers of official arrests for robbery, assault, and total violent felonies were significantly higher for women from high concentration of poverty neighborhoods than for their counterparts in the two other neighborhood subgroups. Significant differences in arrests for these violent crimes among the three neighborhood subgroups remained even after controlling for age, education, marital status, and race. The data also show that 69 percent of the *black* female offenders lived in areas characterized by high concentrations of poverty, whereas only 20 and 11 percent of Hispanic and white women, respectively, lived in such neighborhoods.

These results suggest that, regardless of race, women from high concentration of poverty neighborhoods are involved disproportionately in violent crime. Black women, however, are significantly more likely to reside in these neighborhoods compared to Hispanic or white women. Consequently, it is not surprising to find higher levels of black female involvement in nondomestic violent crimes.

Although the result of our analysis might not be surprising, it is not clear *how* residence in areas characterized by high concentrations of poverty influences women's decisions to participate in crime. Such an understanding requires an exploration of the dynamic processes and structural and economic changes that shape everyday life in New York City's underclass communities. Furthermore, we must ask the question, why now? Why have we seen the escalation of female violence during the past decade (1985–1994)?

Understanding Women's Participation in Violent Street Crime

Our research points to a set of processes that seem to pull inner-city women into violent street crime. Within a community context characterized by economic and social dislocation, growing drug markets, and a marked disappearance of males, situational factors related to family, school, and peer relations combine to create social and economic opportunity structures open to women's increasing participation.

Deindustrialization and Neighborhood Change

The decline in industrial manufacturing in urban areas reshaped the social organization of both conventional and deviant street networks. U.S. cities lost millions of manufacturing jobs beginning in the 1960s (Kasarda, 1988). The flight of jobs led to dramatic shifts in the gender-age composition of inner-city neighborhoods (Wilson, 1987). Traditionally, black people have relied heavily on blue-collar jobs in manufacturing for economic sustenance and social mobility (Farley and Allen, 1987). Manufacturing jobs provided entry positions on career ladders for blacks and Latinos that provided stable if unspectacular earning potential, usually with the expectation of predictable annual increases and a cushion of health and other benefits.

As these jobs disappeared, the ranks of unemployed adult males grew among those remaining in the increasingly poor inner cities (Kasarda, 1989; Tienda, 1989). Unemployment increased and wages decreased among black males from 1970 to 1990 despite a labor-shortage economy (Freeman, 1991; Moss and Tilley, 1991). At least part of the decline in marriage rates may be attributable to the decline in men's "marriage capital" owing to their declining economic fortunes and increased troubles with the law, work, and drugs (Wilson 1987; Mare and Winship 1991; Kirschenman and Neckerman, 1991; Sampson, 1992). In turn, the social networks organized around work grew weaker and generally diminished the role, fortunes, and influence of males in inner cities.

The structural circumstances of women changed as well. Marriage rates, unmarried mothers' employment rates, and the real value of welfare benefits declined simultaneously through the 1980s (Corcoran and Parrott, 1992; Farley, 1988; Mare and Winship, 1991). Marriage rates declined, as did the proportion of adult males to females, and in turn, the percentage of female-headed households (both with and without children) increased from 1970 to 1990 (Jargowsky and Bane, 1990, 1991; Wilson 1987; Wacquant and Wilson, 1989). Many of these households had incomes below the poverty line (Jencks, 1991). The composition changes led to a growing trend in poor neighborhoods in which adolescents "coming up" were as likely to be raised by a poor woman or within a female kinship network as by a household with an adult male (Ricketts and Sawhill, 1988; Jencks 1991; Wacquant and Wilson, 1989).

In addition to declining male wages, there was increased poverty among female-headed households as wages declined for working women with low educational attainment. Employment and wages for black female high school dropouts and unmarried mothers de-

clined sharply in the 1970s, whereas employment and wages increased for married women (Corcoran and Parrott, 1992). Thus,
since job skills became a critical marker of employment success,
manufacturing job losses excluded unskilled black women from
the workforce. The growth of the informal economy in New York
City, including an expanding drug economy, created both motivation and opportunity for unskilled women to participate in the legal and illegal informal enterprises (Sassen-Koob, 1989).

For many young women in inner-city neighborhoods, economic
marginalization is compounded by anxieties concerning their ability to adequately fulfill the social role of mother as well as con-
sumer. These anxieties have heightened during the past decade, in
part because of declining access to financial assistance and the failure of welfare payments to be indexed to inflation (Gans, 1995).

As neighborhoods grew poorer and younger, new female models
emerged to compete with the influences of "female old heads"
(Anderson, 1990). Alongside working women and women in "traditional" roles, the new "heads" displayed the "high life": buying
fancy clothes, jewelry, drugs, and alcohol, while eschewing marriage. Like her male counterpart, the "female old head" traditionally served as important community role models. These women
believed in hard work and family life, and they "repeatedly and in-
sistently told attentive boys and girls 'what was good for them'"
(Anderson, 1990:4). But as meaningful employment became increasingly scarce and drugs and crime became institutionalized in
poor neighborhoods, both male and female "old heads" lost their
prestige and authority. With the expansion of the drug economy
and its opportunities for "crazy money" (Williams, 1989), street-
smart girls (and boys) rejected the "old heads'" lessons about life
and the work ethic.

As family caretakers and role models disappear or decline in influence, and as unemployment and poverty become more persistent, girls looking for direction to achieve a more conventional life
have little direct personal support. The informal social controls of
neighborhoods that help to restrain female initiation into crime,
particularly the traditional pattern of gender role socialization in
which the activities of girls are often monitored more carefully
than those of boys (Hagan et al., 1987), have been eroded. Thus,
changes in population composition and labor-market access may

have weakened the informal controls that regulated crime and drug networks and the people who participated in them.

The economic and social changes enumerated are not the only factors relevant to female participation in violent street crime. The increased supply and demand for cocaine products, especially crack, and the depletion of males in the 20- to 35-year age group removed some of the barriers to female participation in street-level deviance.

The Expansion of the Cocaine Economy

The transition of street drug markets from heroin to cocaine and crack changed the social organization of drug use and selling in New York and other large cities. Street-level drug selling in New York, for example, was a family-centered heroin and marijuana business until the 1980s, when new organizations developed to control cocaine distribution (Johnson, Hamid, and Morales, 1990). Coupled with the structural and contextual changes in street drug networks, changes in drugs and drug markets made possible new avenues and contexts for women to participate in drug use and selling.

First, the increased availability of inexpensive cocaine products, especially cheap smokable cocaine, made possible serious drug use without the risks of injection or physiological addiction (Bourgois, 1989; Hamid, 1990; Waldorf et al., 1991). Cocaine is different from heroin in every way: it is a stimulant rather than a depressant; it is ingested in a variety of ways (nasally, smoked, or injected); and it has a shorter half-life for the high that has motivated many buyers to return for frequent purchases.[3] Moreover, cocaine hydrochloride (HCl), the powder form, was portrayed for many years as a "safe" drug that was not addictive and did not interfere with other social activities and whose use could be easily self-controlled (Siegel, 1987; Waldorf et al., 1991). The ability to use intense drugs without needles and their risk of HIV transmission was an added appeal for some users (Fagan and Chin, 1991; Siegel 1987; Reinarman et al., 1989; Williams, 1992). Accordingly, attractions of the drug itself helped increase demand for safer forms of expensive and intense drug use.

Second, this expansion created demands that exceeded the capacity of older distribution networks (Johnson, Hamid, and Morales,

1990; Fagan, 1992; Baskin et al., 1993). Cocaine products became widely available as drug selling points and organizations grew to meet the expanded demand (Zimmer, 1987; Williams, 1989). The cocaine HCl and crack markets were nurtured by repeat purchases by customers on lengthy sessions often lasting days. This contributed to an extremely active but highly disorganized market. Demand for cocaine products was fueled by its short-lasting effects (an intense high lasting no more than 20 minutes, followed by a sharp "crash" and depression). This psychopharmacological cycle motivated many buyers to return frequently to the street markets "chasing the high." Its relatively low unit cost ($10–20 for a vial with three rocks or $10 for a small packet of powder) and its ease of use (no needles, only a pipe for smoking or tools for snorting) also made cocaine products widely accessible. Entry into drug selling was possible with capital investments of as little as $50.

Third, drug selling became an attractive income option for young people with low education and job skills in a shrinking labor market. Young people in illicit enterprises began to talk about drug selling as "going to work" and the money earned as "getting paid" (Sullivan 1989; Padilla, 1992). Young men and, increasingly, women had several employment options within drug markets: support roles (lookout, steering), manufacturing (cut, package, weigh), or direct street sales (Johnson, Hamid, and Morales, 1990; Goldstein et al., 1991).

The result was an institutionalized cocaine economy, for both cocaine HCl and crack, in New York City. In storefronts, from behind the counters in bodegas, on street corners, in crack or "freak" houses, and through several types of "fronts," drug selling was a common and visible feature of the neighborhoods (Hamid, 1992). Cocaine markets were relatively easy to enter, requiring a capital investment of only a few dollars to create a product for a seemingly endless demand (Fagan and Chin, 1990, 1991). In the late 1980s, law enforcement officials characterized the crack industry as "capitalism gone mad" (*New York Times*, 1989a, 1989b).

The combined effects of the expansion, decentralization, and deregulation of drug markets allowed women to circumvent many of the gender barriers to drug selling and may have simplified their entry into drug use and selling. It was easy and cheap for women users to add cocaine and crack to the repertoire of drugs they used and traded socially. For women users, initiation into drug selling was simplified by the expanded circles of users and the opportunities for selling. For other women, drug selling may have been an extension of illegal careers in hustles such as fraud, larceny, and theft (Johnson et al., 1985; Hunt, 1990; Murphy et al., 1991) and an opportunity to increase crime incomes. Others sought to form organizations, a goal simplified by the new markets. These retail cocaine markets are unregulated, composed of many individual entrepreneurs who work their own areas as they would a private business (Reuter et al., 1990; MacCoun and Reuter, 1992; Hunt, 1990). Informal organizations formed along a freelance model wherein a small group of central players is surrounded by many short-term employees who engage in dealing intermittently.

The Changing Composition of the Inner City

In order to understand *women's* participation in these markets, two important trends regarding the disappearance of significant numbers of males from inner-city neighborhoods need to be noted. For one, the risks of violent death or injury associated with drug selling have resulted in a substantial increase in male mortality. Goldstein et al. (1989), for example, found that 32 percent of 414 homicide events in New York City were related primarily to crack sales. Similarly, the District of Columbia Police Department (Reuter et al., 1990) estimated that 50–80 percent of the killings in recent years have been drug-market-related.

Second, the emergence of crack occurred in an era when crime control ideologies had shifted toward punishment, incapacitation, and retribution (Blumstein et al., 1986). Policy responses to the spread of crack focused on street-level law enforcement efforts using mass arrests to sweep low-level dealers and steerers off the streets. Between 1980 and 1988, the number of drug arrests in New York City (Belenko et al., 1991) increased from 18,521 (40 percent for heroin or other opiates) to 88,641 (44 percent for crack). Data on the criminal justice response to crack (Belenko et al., 1991) suggest that crack arrests are being treated more seriously than other, comparable drug cases. The results suggest that New York City crack cases had a higher probability of pretrial detention, felony indictment, and jail sentence.

The end result is that persons convicted of drug sales, especially of crack, primarily black and Latino men between the ages of 20 and 35 (Bureau of Justice, 1996), now constitute the largest proportion of all inmates entering jails and prisons in New York (Ross & Cohen, 1988). Thus, the risk of being incarcerated or seriously injured as a result of participation in the drug trade appears extremely high. Moreover, the high incidence of incarceration and homicide (Goldstein et al., 1989; Reuter et al., 1990) among young, inner-city, minority males, in the wake of expanded demand for drugs, has provided an opportunity structure for female entry into the informal drug economy.

The effects of these structural changes were evident in the street networks that shaped social patterns of drug use, selling, and crime. The guardianship functions of conventional institutions and social networks were weakened with structural change. The declining status of young men may have diminished their "gatekeeper" and mediating roles in both conventional and street networks in poor neighborhoods. Young women were less likely to be involved in domestic arrangements or crime partnerships with males and increasingly likely to be heads of households. To the extent that these contextual changes altered the gender composition and status of males and females in street networks, the mediating influence of street networks on women's drug and crime involvement was likely to be far weaker than among previous female cohorts.

Social Stress and Cultural Adaptation to Violence

Structural changes have brought increasing inequality into the economy and the lives of men and women who live in the most severely distressed communities. Three interrelated processes of capital disinvestment—residential segregation, racial inequality, and concentration of poverty—have intensified the crime problem in these communities (Hagan, 1994). Economic dislocation has impaired the formation of social resources in distressed communities and families, weakening the guardian function of social networks and indirectly encouraging subcultural adaptations to restricted opportunities.

It is not only the structure of opportunity that is distorted by the class transformation of the inner city. The social perception of this structure is altered, as well. Thus, it is not sufficient to recognize the importance of macrostructural constraints; it is imperative to understand the cultural significance of life in extreme poverty.

Because of experiences with extreme economic marginalization and social isolation in severely distressed neighborhoods, networks of kin, friends, and associates tend to doubt that they can achieve approved societal goals. These self-doubts may exist either because of questions concerning their own capabilities or preparedness or because they perceive severe restrictions imposed by a hostile environment (Wilson, 1991). The consequence is lowered individual and collective feelings of efficacy.

What develops and prevails within this shadow of low expectations, therefore, is an attitude or code that places "respect" above all else (Anderson, 1994). Anderson writes that

the code revolves around the presentation of self. Its basic requirement is the display of a certain predisposition to violence. Accordingly, one's bearing must send the unmistakable if sometimes subtle message to the "next person" in public that one is capable of violence and mayhem when the situation requires it. . . . Physical appearance, including clothes, jewelry and grooming, plays an important part in how a person is viewed. Objects of value show not just a person's taste, but also a willingness to possess things that may require defending. . . . When a person can take something from another and then flaunt it, he gains a certain regard by being the owner, or controller, of that thing. . . . To "get in his face," to take something of value from him, to "dis" him, is to enhance one's own worth. All of which underscores the alienation that permeates the inner-city community. There is a generalized sense that very little respect is to be had and therefore everyone competes to get what affirmation they can from the little that is available. (pp. 88–89)

The issue of respect is thus closely tied to whether a person has an inclination to be violent. In severely distressed communities, particularly among young males and increasingly among females, it is sensed that something essential is at stake in every interaction. People are encouraged to rise to every occasion, particularly with strangers. To run away from such disputes would leave one's self-esteem in tatters.

Thus, the inclination to violence springs from the circumstances of life among the ghetto poor: economic and social marginalization, the stigma of race, the fallout from widespread drug use and drug selling, and the resulting alienation and lack of hope for the future. Living in such an environment tends to expand the range of situations for which violence is perceived as an appropriate and often necessary response. To the extent that people lack hope, they have shorter fuses. They do not see the consequences in the same way. The end result is the formation of a "subculture of angry aggression" (Bernard, 1990), a "code of the streets" (Anderson, 1994) that demands the use of violence to gain respect, enhance self-esteem, and establish reputations.

In communities depleted of economic and social resources, young women have created their own version of "manhood" (Anderson, 1994). Their goal is the same: to get respect, to be recognized as capable of setting or maintaining a certain standard. These women confronted with a "sea of destitution" attempt to "recapitalize" (Hagan, 1994) their lives by investing in the value of public posturing and the use of violence.

Notes

1. Wilson argued that one of the major factors involved in the growth of ghetto poverty is the occurrence of industrial restructuring (shift from goods-producing to service-producing industries, relocation of manufacturing industries out of the central city) and labor-market swings (polarization of the labor market into low-wage and high-wage sectors, wage stagnation, periodic recessions). Another factor is the out-migration of higher income residents from certain parts of the inner city, resulting in a higher concentration of residents in extreme poverty or living in ghetto neighborhoods.

2. We used the most recent address since that location compared positively with (i.e., was equivalent to) other neighborhoods identified in the women's residential histories.

3. The psychoactive and physiological effects of cocaine are quite different from those of heroin. Cocaine is a short-acting central nervous system stimulant. Cocaine blocks the reabsorption of dopamine, a neurotransmitter chemical, into the neurons that release it. It thereby temporarily accelerates perception and thoughts. Cocaine is powerfully reinforcing, and both animals and humans who find that a given behavior will lead to a dose of cocaine will increase the frequency of that behavior (Gawin, 1991). Whereas heroin use involved a small number of consistent daily doses, cocaine and crack use were characterized by multiple purchases in

relatively short periods of time. The psychoactive effects of heroin and methods of administration limited the volume of sales and the number of users. Cocaine effects are relatively short-lived, and the declining stimulation of pleasure centers leads to anxiety, edginess, and depression (Waldorf et al., 1991). Users can ward off the effects of this "crash" by using more cocaine. Thus, cocaine sessions often entail binges of many hours (sleeping is obviated) of repeated use. The effects of smoking crack or cocaine freebase are more intense but similar. Reports from users suggested that smoking a rock of crack produced a brief (about 20 minutes) but intense high, followed by a "crash" and the rapid onset of depression, with a compelling drive to get high again (Spitz and Rosecan, 1997; Siegel, 1987; Reinarman et al., 1989; Fagan and Chin, 1991).

Chapter Three

Getting into Crime and Violence

Everyone's life has its ups and downs, traumas, losses, and sadness. Almost all children have some trouble with their families, schools, and peers (Pipher, 1994). Many girls, some of whom have gone on to become famous (Georgia O'Keeffe, Margaret Mead, Maya Angelou, to name a few), experienced rejection and social isolation while they were growing up (Kerr, 1985). In order to weather these experiences, children have relied on feelings of love and safety that at least some institution, either their families, friends, neighbors, or schools, provided. Further, they have counted on futures that would be filled with meaningful work, challenges, and respect. And as Mary Pipher has stated, they felt that they were "part of something larger than their own lives and that they [were] emotionally connected to a whole" (1994:284).

Unfortunately, the women we interviewed lacked both the prosocial and the protective factors found in other communities, schools, and families. By and large, they grew up in neighborhoods characterized by persistent and serious violence, drug dealing, prostitution, and decay; their schools were hard-pressed to keep them safe, interested, and nurtured; they grew up in multiproblem families in which domestic physical and sexual violence was commonplace, drug and alcohol addiction present, and family histories of criminality rampant. As a result, the women we interviewed were bereft of a safe space in which to grow, test ideas, make decisions about their sexuality, appearance, and interests. Instead, they experienced early childhood sexual and physical abuse as well as losses of significant others from premature deaths, alcoholism, mortal violence, and incarceration; these women witnessed, daily, the ravages of growing up in communities that lacked prospects for productive futures. We saw the effects of their backgrounds in their faces and body language; we heard them talk about them during the interviews, and we were touched by the feelings of hopelessness that characterized their dreams.

In this chapter, we share with you the accounts given to us by these women. The women describe their neighborhoods and their experiences in schools, in their families, among peers, and with their initiation into drugs.

The Distressed Community

The decisions these women made about their lives—whether to invest in schooling or vocational training or whether to seek income through legitimate work or crime—did not develop in a vacuum. These choices began to be made while they were growing up, and they were defined, in many ways, by the resources of their communities and families.

The communities in which these women were raised suffered severely from capital disinvestment. Their families had few network resources and little social capital to facilitate investment in their children. Furthermore, these communities suffered from serious social isolation, with many of its residents lacking real stakes in conformity to conventional society. As a result, these communities lacked the ability to exert sufficient social control over their youth; and these women, along with many of their peers, drifted into cultural adaptations that brought short-term status, material benefits, and a lack of concern over society's evaluation of the methods used to obtain them.

It is important to note here that we are not at all arguing that the women developed an "oppositional culture" (Anderson, 1994; Bourgois, 1995). Such a perspective argues that offenders *consciously* chose criminality in order to rebel against mainstream aspirations and values. Instead, we are suggesting that for these women, the choices that they made were frequently based only on what they were exposed to in their environment. They did not seem concerned about mainstream society's labeling of their behavior. For that matter, all but one woman refused to define their illegal behaviors as "criminal." Instead, they saw their conduct as "it is what it is," no more, no less. Further, they stated that they did not experience ostracism or any other negative sanctions from family members, neighbors, or other community members. Therefore, why would they see their behaviors as beyond the pale? Although the "pale" may not have *condoned* their offending, it appeared not to have the political, social, or economic resources to do much about it. Much the same could be said of their families. And much *was* said, by these women, about the roles played by their communities and families during their childhoods.

Research on the community context of crime posits that the neighborhoods themselves directly influence behavior, attitudes, values, and opportunities (Bursik and Grasmick, 1993; Harrell and Peterson, 1992; Sampson and Lauritsen, 1994; Wilson, 1987). Community contexts shape what can be termed "cognitive landscapes" (Sampson and Lauritsen, 1994) regarding appropriate standards and expectations of conduct. That is, in severely distressed communities, it appears that a system of values emerges in which violence is not vigorously condemned and is often expected as a routine part of everyday life. These neighborhood-structured perceptions and tolerances in turn appear to influence the probability of violent encounters.

But what were their neighborhoods like while these women were growing up? This section introduces the neighborhoods and describes their ecology and demography using both census and life history data.

Like many other neighborhoods in New York, Washington Heights and Central Harlem, in Manhattan, and Bushwick, in Brooklyn, changed rapidly between 1960 and 1980. Prior to this time period, manufacturing sectors provided stable and predictable income at levels sufficient to sustain families across generations. However, beginning in the late 1960s and continuing at full speed during the 1970s, labor surpluses in inner cities increased. This increase was created by a slowdown in the manufacturing sector and the relocation of remaining jobs to "satellite cities" in surrounding suburbs or regions. The results wreaked havoc on communities that were already economically vulnerable. For instance, between 1970 and 1980, the number of blue-collar and clerical jobs in New York declined by over 350,000 but increased by over 75,000 in the surrounding suburbs and other regions, nationally and internationally. Technical and managerial jobs in the city increased by over 250,000 during this time and by over 400,000 in the suburbs (Kasarda, 1989).

These changes reflected broader structural changes in New York City and other large U.S. metropolitan areas. At the same time, and perhaps fueled by the huge gaps left in the social and economic fabric of these communities, there was a succession of overlapping drug crises. The same neighborhoods that were most affected by the economic and social crises just mentioned were also bombarded by the destabilizing effects of heroin, cocaine (powder), and crack markets. As a result, the formal and informal social controls that at one time had limited crime and regulated drug use and selling were deteriorating.

In Table 3.1, we provide data that are specific to Washington Heights, Central Harlem, and Bushwick. As you will see, by 1980 these neighborhoods had become prototypes of what are referred to as "underclass" communities. [1]

Washington Heights

Beginning in the mid-1800s and continuing for a long time after, Washington Heights was home to German immigrants. During the 1930s, many Jews fleeing Nazi persecution also settled in Washington Heights, giving this neighborhood the nickname Frankfurt-on-the-Hudson. The 1940s brought an influx of stable working-class blacks who left Harlem to settle into the brownstones and houses along Riverside Drive and Sugar Hill. And through the 1950s, working-class immigrant families from Ireland, Germany, Russia, and Poland dominated this neighborhood.

By 1960, Washington Heights had witnessed tremendous demographic changes. Germans accounted for only 16 percent of its residents. Instead, Puerto Rican and Dominican families, also working-class, moved in, as white and black residents who could afford to were moving to the suburbs. The non-Hispanic white population of Washington Heights declined by 32 percent from 1970 to 1980, and another 10 percent from 1980 to 1990. Hispanics replaced non-Hispanic whites at a 1:1 ratio during this period. By 1990, 41 percent of the documented residents of Washington Heights were

TABLE 3.1 Neighborhood Social and Demographic Characteristics, 1970–1980

	Washington Heights			Central Harlem			Bushwick		
	1970	1980	1990	1970	1980	1990	1970	1980	1990
Population	180,710	179,941	198,192	159,336	105,794	105,377	136,770	108,605	119,240
Age (%)									
1–4 years	6.3	9.5	6.7	7.6	6.8	8.5	12.1	11.0	10.3
5–17 years	15.9	15.7	19.2	21.8	16.7	20.3	18.5	20.1	22.4
18–44 years	35.3	41.2	45.2	35.6	35.4	23.0	27.7	29.0	31.2
45 years and older	42.5	33.6	28.6	35.0	41.1	38.2	42.0	40.1	36.4
Ethnicity (%)									
Non-Hispanic white	60.3	28.7	18.8	2.0	0.6	2.1	35.5	15.6	5.7
Non-Hispanic black	12.7	14.5	11.5	94.6	94.1	87.6	27.9	26.4	25.1
Hispanic	25.7	54.6	66.8	3.3	4.4	10.2	35.8	56.8	64.6
Unemployment (%)									
Males	4.3	9.7	13.0	7.9	10.2	21.9	5.6	15.2	15.8
Females	5.0	8.6	13.8	7.5	9.9	17.8	8.0	14.3	16.4
Education: Persons 25+ with < high school education (%)	47.4	51.3	29.0	67.8	57.2	33.4	75.2	68.3	30.1
Family composition: husband-wife (%)	76.8	59.5	45.0	56.7	40.6	37.5	63.4	49.7	41.4
Poverty: families below poverty level (%)	8.8	23.9	11.7	22.9	34.5	29.5	22.8	45.4	15.9
Concentration of poverty (%)									
Census tracts 20% poverty	13.3	60.6	76.7	44.0	69.0	78.0	75.9	96.7	96.7
Census tracts 40% poverty	0.0	6.1	13.3	4.0	32.0	50.2	3.5	80.0	46.7
Census tracts underclass	0.0	0.0	6.7	6.0	13.0	29.0	0.0	56.7	20.0

SOURCES: John Kasarda, 1993. *Urban Underclass Data Base 1960–90.* Chapel Hill, NC: University of North Carolina. New York City Department of City Planning, 1993. *Socioeconomic Profiles 1970–90.* New York: Department of Planning.

Dominican, and many more residents were illegal and therefore nonregistered immigrants from the Dominican Republic.

In large part owing to the extremely high percentage of immigrants in the community, educational attainment for Washington Heights residents is low compared to that of other parts of New York City including Manhattan. Almost 1 out of 2 adult residents does not have a high school education. Low levels of educational attainment are reflected in the types of jobs that are most common among residents: sales and technical support jobs, especially clerical work, followed by service jobs and positions as operators and laborers.

New York City's long economic recession and restructuring of the economy have weakened further the labor market in Washington Heights. Many residents have been displaced from light manufacturing, especially the garment industry, and now find jobs only in the lower paying service sector (Duany, 1994). Many of these skilled workers survive by selling food on the street, driving gypsy cabs, or taking other temporary work in the informal economy.

It is important to note, too, that the unemployment rate over the past two decades has been consistently higher in Washington Heights than in the rest of Manhattan or New York City and has continued to increase among residents, even as it began to decrease in New York City. In 1970, 4 percent of the males and 5 percent of the females were unemployed. By 1980, the unemployment rate was 10 percent and 9 percent, respectively, for males and females. And by 1990, official unemployment rose to over 13 percent each for males and females, a figure likely to be conservative in neighborhoods with concentrations of recent immigrants (Sassen-Koob, 1989).

In addition, during the period of 1970 to 1990, poverty grew and became more concentrated. The percentage of census tracts with 20 percent poverty rates rose from 13 percent in 1970 to 60.6 percent in 1980 and to 77 percent by 1990. By 1990, one in three Washington Heights residents lived in poverty.

During this period, Washington Heights experienced a notable increase in female-headed families with children. The percentage of two-parent families decreased from 52 percent to 45 percent during the 1980s. Poverty was acute among female-headed families with children under 18: In 1970, 31 percent lived in poverty, whereas by 1980 the percentage rose to 59 percent. By 1990, we were able to see the real effects of the increasing concentration of poverty over this time period. For families with children under the age of 5, 45 percent lived in poverty, and for female-headed families with children under 18, 64 percent lived in poverty. In 1990, at least 46 percent of Washington Heights children lived in poverty, compared to 36 percent in Manhattan and 30 percent citywide.

Amid these economic and social changes, drug dealing took hold in Washington Heights in the early 1980s. It exploded with the introduction of crack in the mid-1980s. About the same time, the streets of Washington Heights were besieged by violence. Homicides, many of which were drug-related, were clustered in Washington Heights. Further, Washington Heights consistently accounted for the most homicides in Manhattan. And with every passing year, residents have told us, there are more drugs, more crime, more guns, more death.

People on the streets of Washington Heights are exposed to the drug economy and violence even if they do not participate in it. For example, during one of our walks through the neighborhood, we noticed funeral wreaths and memorial candles in front of a brick building, No. 505. It was obvious that someone had died there. Death appeared to be a regular visitor to this block. Painted on the side of building 505 was a black and gray mural of a cemetery. Listed on it were the names of the dead from the neighborhood, 51 in all. There was space for plenty more. As we crossed the street, youths leaning against the wall asked if we wanted anything. Drugs, from crack to heroin, is what they had in mind.

Our short walk highlighted the grim realities of a neighborhood betrayed by the passage of time. Although most residents have nothing to do with drugs and violence, they are on the defensive. The drug dealers and street hustlers have managed to set the tone for public life. Perhaps most important, they provide a persuasive, though violent, alternative lifestyle to mainstream society.

Central Harlem

Central Harlem is an area of some 1,000 acres in the north-central part of the borough of Manhattan. Since the early 1900s, its population has been overwhelmingly black. Central Harlem in 1980 remained a homogeneously African-American community that had become much poorer in the preceding decade. Over one-third of its population was lost during the 1970s, whereas the percentage of families with incomes below poverty levels grew to over one in three. When adjusted for inflation, median income for families decreased by almost 25 percent over the decade; the decline was nearly 50 percent for unrelated individuals. More than one in five families (22.5 percent) were receiving public assistance in 1980. In all of the 29 census tracts, more than 20 percent of the population had incomes below the poverty line, a common threshold for designation as a poverty tract.

The straightforward problem of finding a job was a serious one for Central Harlem residents during the decade of the 1970s. During the 1970s, unemployment ranged from a low of 7 percent, for males aged 20–44, to a high of 30 percent, for males aged 16–19. Of those Harlem residents who did work, many held marginal jobs, often employed only part-time. Over one-third of the workers were employed in unskilled jobs, typically earning poverty wages. The Labor Department's "subemployment rate" for Central Harlem, a measure designed to capture these hidden aspects of the unemployment problem in a single index, was estimated at 39.4 percent in 1980. This means that 4 out of 10 members of the Harlem labor force manifested a substandard employment status in 1980.

Central Harlem also experienced large demographic shifts during the 1970s. The percentage of married couples declined significantly in this period, but the percentage of single-parent families (primarily female-headed households) grew by only 4 percent. By 1985, however, over 80 percent of all births were out of wedlock in Central Harlem.

Much of Central Harlem's housing stock was built during the period from 1870 through the first decade of the twentieth century. During the 1970s, over 10 percent of the housing units were considered dilapidated—unfit for human occupancy. Another 40 percent were deteriorating. More recently, a *Daily News* (1994) article focused on one block in Central Harlem, describing West 140th Street as a wasteland: "Twenty-two of the 36 buildings had been abandoned to city control. Eight were boarded up. The rest were in disrepair. Windows are broken, hallways are a mosaic of peeling paint and broken plaster" (p. 12).

The voices of 140th Street tell the story, as quoted in the following: "It's like we live in a twilight zone, there's no sense of community, no sense of nothing. It's like a war zone, we have accepted death like we do in a third world country—it's out of control" (*New York Times*, 1994).

A 1978 *New York* magazine article underscored what life was like for the women in our study who grew up in Central Harlem:

It's New York's most wicked zone—a square mile of urban badland known to law enforcement officials in the area as Dodge City. . . . Over the last four years, 360 men, women, and children have been shot, knifed, beaten, bludgeoned, or otherwise battered to death. . . . Hardly a week goes by without gunfire in the streets, without people diving for cover, without victims crumbling to the ground. Rapes, robberies and assaults are commonplace. Fear is the way it is. (Young, 1978:44)

A major part of street life for the women growing up in Central Harlem was the availability of drugs and guns. They were as easy to come by (and continue to be) as cigarettes or candy. On a recent visit, we witnessed a man on the corner of 145th and Eighth Avenue who openly advertised to passersby (including the authors) a new .38 caliber revolver he had clumsily concealed in a brown paper bag under his arm. Drugs and guns are available in bars, poolrooms, and candy stores and on the streets. They were and are available everywhere.

Bushwick

The 1960s were a time of rapid changes in the population of many neighborhoods in Brooklyn. In Bushwick, a large influx of Hispanics, mostly from Puerto Rico, began to displace the ethnic enclaves that had dominated neighborhoods in northern Brooklyn. It was not until the 1970s and 1980s that Dominicans and other Hispanics began to move there in large numbers. The percentage of non-Hispanic whites declined from 36 percent in 1970 to 16 percent in 1980 and to 6 percent in 1990, whereas the percentage of Latinos increased from 36 percent in 1970 to 57 percent in 1980 and to 65 percent in 1990.

"Blockbusting" activities by real estate speculators began the flight of whites from Bushwick. Their exodus signaled the beginning of a long period of disinvestment, abandonment of buildings and high vacancy rates, arson, and drug-related crime. By the late

1970s, the process of ghettoization was nearly complete. The long period of devastation peaked in the 1977 New York City blackout, during which Bushwick was the most severely ravaged neighborhood in the city. By 1992, one-fifth of the zoned lots in Bushwick lay vacant.

Since the 1960s, Bushwick has been a relatively poor neighborhood (23 percent of families lived below the poverty line in 1970); by 1980, it was severely distressed. Nearly half (46 percent) of the families had incomes below the poverty level, and 69 percent of female-headed households with children lived in poverty by 1980. Official unemployment rates among both males and females exceeded 15 percent by 1980, representing a 171 percent and 79 percent increase from 1970 for males and females, respectively.

The growing concentration of poverty in Bushwick also is reflected in the percentage of census tracts that meet each of three poverty definitions: at least 20 percent of the population below poverty, at least 40 percent of the population below poverty, and tracts defined as "underclass" (Ricketts and Sawhill 1988). For example, using the broadest definition of 20 percent of the population below poverty, Table 3.1 shows that poverty rose dramatically in the 1970s in Bushwick. Nearly all the Bushwick tracts had 20 percent of their population below poverty by 1980. The percentage of "underclass" census tracts, the most restrictive classification, rose from none in Bushwick in 1970 to over half (56.7 percent) in 1980, and it remained at stable high rates in 1990.

Despite the relative homogeneity of the Hispanic population from the 1960s until the 1980s, this group was unable to make any significant steps toward organizing themselves as a political force to be reckoned with. Without legitimate forms of political power and representation within their reach, some Hispanics in Bushwick found that drug distribution was a route not only to wealth, but also to economic and political power. Hilga, an old-time resident, noted that established distributors in Bushwick—"owners"—possessed vast wealth and property within the neighborhood. They were clearly well integrated into the community. Her account of the first curbside distributor ended with the observation that he had built himself up from being nearly penniless to owning a "fleet of cars" and many buildings in the neighborhood. She went on to describe how the area lacked many types of neighborhood organi-

zations that existed in other parts of Brooklyn, and that many families were involved in the drug business.

> We never had any block associations. No, not in this neighborhood.
> This neighborhood wasn't together. One reason, I think, is because a
> lot of these people had a son or somebody bringing in some type of
> [illegally earned] money. Even *grandmothers* used to be lookouts.
> Whole families used to be into selling drugs. Yeah, from the 70s on;
> when they started selling drugs in the streets, they needed lookouts.
> It was like a family affair.

Hilga's account suggests that the lack of participation in formal
organizations among neighborhood residents was partially com-
pensated for by the existence of family-based drug distribution
networks and that these family-based organizations acted as
springboards to political and economic power within the neighborhood.

Bushwick, like nearly every neighborhood in northern Brooklyn
during the 1960s and 1970s, had a variety of spots where local residents could purchase heroin, cocaine, marijuana, and other drugs.
Many of these were indoor locations—bars, bodegas, pool halls,
apartments—where a personal connection to the dealer was necessary to obtain access. Viva, a longtime heroin user, talks about the
relative discreetness of street-level drug markets before the 1980s:

> At that time [1970s], they wouldn't sell drugs in the street too much.
> You would have to go like to a house. At that time there was black
> and Spanish guys selling it. Years ago they used to sell drugs in a bar
> on Halsey Street. You go there, right, and they would sell to you. And
> then they had a house connection across the street from the bar. If
> they didn't know you, they wouldn't sell. It's a lot different today.
> They'll sell to anybody.

Outdoor sales of drugs during this period were mostly confined
to public parks. There was virtually no trafficking on residential
streets. Though street-level drug markets had been present in
Bushwick for many years, it was not until the mid-1980s that they
began to expand dramatically and attract distributors and con-
sumers from surrounding neighborhoods. This development
should be viewed in light of citywide changes in street-level drug
markets during this period, wherein the process of market shrink-

age in some neighborhoods led to the growth and intensification in others. Crack markets in central and northern Brooklyn generally began to shrink beginning in 1988. The result of this overall shrinkage in Brooklyn crack markets was the emergence of an ethnically heterogeneous street-level drug supermarket in Bushwick.

By the late 1980s there was a visible increase in the number of street-level distributors in the neighborhood. At the same time, there was an increase in the number of street-level drug users, many coming from other neighborhoods. These users would come to Bushwick in order to take advantage of the quality and greater availability of drugs in Bushwick compared with other nearby neighborhoods.

Hope, a 43-year-old African-American from Bedford Stuyvesant reported the following:

> Over here there was much more people, you know. Troutman is open all night long and stuff. It's like a 42nd Street. My friend said there are some good drugs here. And I have to admit, the drugs were good.

By 1990, Bushwick was transformed into a mecca for drug distribution and use, and violence was the currency of social control.

A picture emerges of three communities in which capital and public disinvestment processes have made economic prospects bleak and weakened community social networks and the social capacities of families and in which crime has become a short-term adaptive effort to "recapitalize" (Hagan, 1994) the lives of individuals and communities. Yet these numbers do not capture how these women *perceived* the concentration effects of increasing impoverishment.

During our interviews with these women, conversation turned to the neighborhoods in which they grew up. We were interested in getting their impressions of several facets of everyday life. We began with issues related to what Skogan called "physical decay" (1990). We asked the women, "When visualizing the community in which you grew up, what scenes come to mind?" The vast majority of the women saw abandoned housing, rundown buildings, and streets filled with trash.

These signs of physical disorder are important aspects of community life in that they "stigmatize it [the community] in the eyes of residents and outsiders alike" (Skogan, 1990:36), affecting morale and feelings of control. Further, they symbolize, in very concrete ways, society's disinvestment in this community. Abandoned and rundown housing and erratic trash removal are indications that local governments, landlords, and business people do not see enough value to tear down or renovate the structures, open new housing units or businesses, or ensure the health and safety of the residents by removing the trash. Instead, these buildings and garbage heaps are used for drug transactions and use and as hangouts for the homeless, psychiatrically distressed, and those engaged in "trouble."

Social Disorder

In addition to physical disorder, the women recounted their childhood memories of rampant "social disorder" (Skogan, 1990). Again, the vast majority of women remembered streets teaming with prostitutes, winos and junkies, delinquent youth, and late-night partyers. Most feared for their personal safety and recalled many instances when they observed their friends and neighbors getting hurt during street quarrels. They reported that muggings were a routine occurrence in their immediate neighborhoods, as were displays of weapons, which were often used in street fights. At least half of the women felt that homicides were *not* unusual and that theft and drug abuse were common.

Stephanie, who grew up in Central Harlem, provided us with the following description:

Steppin' out of my building you would always see, uh, men cussing around the liquor store, drinking wine. There was always, uh, drugs in the neighborhood. It was dope. Mostly dope. I seen a lot of dope. I seen people layin' in the building after they been mugged. You know, blood and stuff around. I see people shooting up in the hallways. It was a lot of fightin' in the neighborhood too. Sure, violence and a lot of fightin' goin' on and cussin' and fightin' and cutting, lots of knives.

I was always frightened. I was scared. And even when I ran with the gangs, I was, I was scared to death of guns. I remember playin' hooky one time in the park. We were drinking and this guy put the pistol to my head. I didn't know whether it was loaded or not. I just remember looking in the barrel, and I almost passed out. I almost passed out I was so scared. When I was growing up it was important not to be an accident. A lot was goin' on. Kids gettin' shot accidentally, guys playin' with guns. And you just become a statistic. It was an accident, and I remember never wantin' to be an accident.

When I was running the streets, I guess, I guess part of the thrill was an element of danger. I liked it. I liked it. And the time there was an element of danger, I was with it. But I still, I was scared, sure. But that, that, I guess that was part of the fun.

The disorder apparent in these neighborhoods was indicative of a decline in community self-control. Fear, demoralization, and eventually resignation seemed characteristic of these women's responses to life in the neighborhoods. Over time, these women developed a blasé attitude toward the violence that surrounded them. And eventually, for these women, it became part of an accepted mode of functioning. Jocorn's account of street life in Bushwick epitomizes how violence was part of the women's "common-sense" realities:

Well I was raised up in Brooklyn, and Brooklyn was like, um, it's like okay to see a whole bunch of people on the train druggin', and you know, uh, the cops pass them by, and they won't have much to say about it. In the night it was like lookin' out the window, and it was okay to see somebody get ripped off. Or somebody pop out of a car and shoot somebody. That was like an everyday thing. In the park, uh, they would do like, you know, block parties. There was not a block party that I didn't go to that I didn't see somebody get shot or something like that. Or you have a incident where a man just picked a child and attempted to throw her out the window. I seen people jump out of windows, you know.

Growing up in these neighborhoods meant that any time spent on the streets or looking down from a window meant exposure to violence, even if one was not a participant. The pervasiveness and extreme forms of violence witnessed and often experienced by these women led them to interpret and accept violence as "not a big thing," as an expected outcome of neighborhood life. Darlene provides us with this account:

Oh, yeah, I've definitely been assaulted in my neighborhood while growing up, even raped. I was shoved back inside my door by a neighbor in the next building. And, uh, that's when I got a fractured jaw. A knife was put to my throat and I was raped. I've had my share of assaults, but that's part of growing up there. That's all it is.

Here, Denise nonchalantly describes life in Central Harlem:

When I walked out of my house I saw a sick, depressing, ugly bunch
of bullshit. I think it was somewhat safe in the daytime. At night it
became ours, and you either knew how to deal or you didn't. You
could get stuck up, you could get beat, you could get cut, you could
get raped. Violence was everywhere. I was raped by three of my
classmates. I was robbed twice. I've had black eyes, a fractured jaw. A
knife was put to my throat. Drug dealing was the pretty side. The
pretty side. If you became a well-known drug dealer and you were
good, you got the utmost respect.

These particular accounts of growing up in Bushwick, Washington Heights, and Central Harlem are not aberrations. They are visible reflections of the social and economic crises that are concentrated in these neighborhoods. In these neighborhoods, in order to
have some involvement in the "pretty side," young people, both
men and women, have become involved in a variety of serious and
potentially lethal criminal activities. For many of these young people, the standards of the "street code" (Anderson, 1994) are perceived as the only way to gain respect and establish reputations.

One might ask, though, where are the parents of these young
people? Can't their families and home environments protect them
from the ravages of the streets? Unfortunately, many families that
previously could provide instrumental and emotional support
were affected dramatically by capital disinvestment and the expansion of drug abuse and sales. Thus, for the majority of women in
our sample, the home did not provide a respite from violence, aggression, and dysfunction.

The Distressed Family

Families exist as part of a *web* of social institutions that influence
the behavior of members. As part of a network, families are affected by their access to a larger set of resources that provide economic, political, and social opportunities and formal and informal
behavioral controls. Many of these processes were described previously as being part of the neighborhood context.

However, families also exert influence through their own set of
processes that are related to and affected by the broader structure.
For example, families perform instrumental functions that provide

for the health and welfare of their members. Thus, the extent to which a family has access to income, housing, food, health care, and clothing, it is performing its instrumental function. Families also have expressive functions. The extent to which the family fosters relationships of love and affection, emotional stability, a sense of belonging, self-esteem, and dignity, it is performing its expressive functions. Furthermore, families either tend toward being "decent," that is, they "accept mainstream values and instill them in their children" (Anderson, 1994:82), or they are "street" in that they are "disorganized," self-destructive (e.g., addicted, violent), and socialize their children in the code of the streets (Anderson, 1994:83).

Unfortunately, families in neighborhoods such as those just described are less likely to meet their instrumental or expressive functions and, at best, attempt to approximate "decent" families but are more likely to be "street." Communities such as Central Harlem, Washington Heights, and Bushwick lack the necessary economic and political resources to generate socially approved opportunities, and they are unable to cultivate the appropriate cultural controls to neutralize the attraction of illegitimate opportunities.

It is within this context that inner-city families struggle to offset the draw to criminal behavior that pulls at their children. Unfortunately, many families fail. Their desperation and inability to manage the demands placed on them make it difficult for them to balance their own needs for control and catharsis with those of other family members (Anderson, 1994). As a result, children in "street" families grow up in families that are full of anger, frustration, aggression, and deviance.

Several specific family processes have been identified as being related to participation in violent street crime and also to life within "street families." They include the presence of physical and sexual abuse (Alfaro, 1978; Lewis et al., 1979; Groth, 1979; Potts, Herzberger, and Holland, 1979; Geller and Ford-Somma, 1984; Guarino, 1985); mental illness and drug and alcohol abuse (Cocozza, 1980; Anderson, 1994); inadequate or inappropriate parental supervision (Cernkovich and Giordano, 1987; Matsueda and Heimer, 1987; Loeber and Stoudthamer-Loeber, 1986; Patterson and Dishion, 1985; Farrington, 1978; Hirschi, 1969); and criminal involvement of other family members (Owens and Straus, 1975; McCord, 1979; Simcha-Fagan and Silver, 1982; Fagan et al., 1983).

Although the strength and directness of these relationships are still being explored, there appears to be consensus that family processes do indeed have an impact on children's socialization toward violence.

The women we interviewed described a family environment in which there was an overconcentration of these negative processes. For instance, 40 percent of the women we interviewed reported that while growing up they were *severely and regularly* beaten by a family member. This comes as no surprise since an association between high rates of child abuse and serious criminality, especially among the urban poor, has been found in previous research (Fagan and Wexler, 1987; Straus et al., 1980). It should be noted here that *witnessing* acts of abuse also has the deleterious consequences associated with victimization (Sorrells, 1977; Lewis et al., 1979; Hartstone and Hansen, 1984). As you will see, the witnessing of violence was about as routine an experience for these women as brushing the teeth is for others.

But the abuse was not limited to beatings. Thirty-six percent of the women we spoke to were sexually abused by a member of their immediate family, and 26 percent were sexually abused by someone in their extended family. These types of sexual assaults, that is, assaults by family members, especially when the victim is young, tend to produce the most trauma (Pipher, 1994:220). In addition, the resulting trauma is exacerbated when the victim feels she has no one to confide in, to turn to for help, or to provide her with support as she deals with her rage, resentment, and anger. Unfortunately, the women in our study routinely reported that they grew up in an environment in which they felt unprotected and alone in having to deal with the aftermath of abuse.

The distress experienced by family members and witnessed by the women did not end with abuse. Of the women with whom we spoke, 34 percent told us that during their childhood, at least one member of their immediate family was hospitalized for a mental health reason. Typically, the patient was the respondent's mother or sister. Further, 69 percent of the women had a parent or sibling who had been arrested at some point while they were growing up. Many others reported family involvement in street crime, typically drug dealing, that did not end in an arrest. The presence of criminal behavior within the family unit provided these women with routine exposure to and socialization toward the tolerance of illegal behavior.

It should be noted, as well, that 72 percent of the women came from families with serious alcohol problems, and 86 percent lived with at least one member of their family who was drug-addicted. One cannot underestimate the impact of drug and alcohol abuse on family processes. Studies have demonstrated a strong relationship between parental substance abuse and hostile family relations (Dunlap, 1992). And research has pointed to the dissolution of protective family networks and practices as a result of such abuse (Anderson, 1990; Johnson, Williams, et al., 1990; Dunlap, 1992; Loeber and Wikstrom, 1993). The disruption of positive family practices has also been associated with high rates of crime and delinquency, especially violent offending (Sampson and Groves, 1989; Sampson, 1986; Felson and Cohen, 1980; Felson, 1986).

It is important to note that these women were growing up during a 20-year period of time, the mid-1960s to mid-1980s, when drug addiction took a terrible toll on their neighborhoods, exacerbating already deteriorating social, economic, and familial networks. Beginning with heroin and culminating with the most ravaging drug—crack—the already vulnerable communities, schools, and families in which the women lived were racked by the effects of addiction. And notably, the effects were most pronounced in black and Hispanic families. The extended family networks that once acted to stave off disaster and provide for the instrumental and expressive needs of its members were taxed by the ways in which addiction sucked at its lifeblood; and for blacks and Hispanics, the result was a growing dissolution of these networks (Tucker and Mitchell-Kernan, 1995). Many children growing up at this time, especially those with addicted parents, had nowhere to turn for support and guidance. They experienced intense loneliness, difficulties in school (Sowder and Burt, 1980), and increasing isolation from conventional and prosocial activities. And consistently they were warned to keep family "business" and problems to themselves.

You can hear the pain, rage, and loneliness as the women we spoke to tell us their stories. Barbara, a black woman who grew up in Bushwick during the 1960s and early 70s, recounts a life that was typical of the women with whom we spoke:

My mother and father lived together. But my mother was, uh, like the father and the mother. She was the strength of the house 'cause my father was an alcoholic. And, uh, he was just a little wimp. He was no help to my mother at all. All he did was cause a lot of trouble and heartaches. He's been arrested a few times, drunken driving, messing, fighting policemen.

Uh, the fact that my father was an alcoholic when I was growing up really didn't seem like anything was wrong with that 'cause most of the people I lived around's fathers was alcoholics, or they didn't have a father in the family. So, it wasn't out of the ordinary.

My mother and father, they fought all of the time. As a matter of fact, my father tried to kill my mother with a knife. Even when I was real little, I remember my mother having to hit my father in the head in order to stop him. My mother used to be afraid of my father. And there were times when she really had to stand up with him. At one time, he used to make broomsticks. They were called super broomsticks. And she bopped him in the head with the super broomstick.

But she always would take him back, though. They would separate, and then she would take him back. And he would get drunk, and he would mess around with other women.

And, it would be unusual to open up the refrigerator and don't see beer or something inside, or people coming over on weekdays, uh, to have parties, and seeing people drunk and falling down and fights. You know it seemed too normal.

I also have three brothers and four sisters. My brother, Billy, he's been arrested—robbery on the trains. My sister's out there on the street. My baby brother does cocaine, crack, and alcohol. The other brother is an alcoholic whether he wants to believe it or not. My brother Gary, too. My sister is a crack addict, an alcoholic, a garbage head. She's also been in a mental hospital.

My mother wasn't the type you could sit down and talk to. She always screamed and yelled about the things she wanted. There were times that I did want to go to her, but I was afraid because of her reaction. She didn't know how to really talk to her children. Whenever I would get in trouble or something, I wouldn't go to her.

But growing up like this wasn't so strange, it didn't seem so wrong cause most people had families like that.

Janelle provides us with a similar, although less vivid account:

My mother and grandmother raised me. I have one brother and one sister. Both of them are younger. I have lots of cousins. All of my cousins have been incarcerated, mostly for robbery. I used to be at my aunt's with them all of the time. I was also molested by most of my cousins as I was growing up.

My mother never said anything about my getting high because she drank herself.

I have one brother and one sister. We moved a lot but always to the same type of place. My parents lived together until I was 16 and then they tied the knot. Then they separated a year later and they never lived together again. And then my father died, a year after they separated.

My father was an alcoholic, and he smoked marijuana and he sniffed cocaine.

As hard as it is for most of us to believe, growing up in a household replete with domestic violence (physical, sexual, or both), an alcoholic father, an emotionally absent mother, sibling criminality, substance abuse, and mental health problems was the norm for the women in our study. Take Monica's account of her family while growing up:

I have six sisters and two brothers. My brother Victor, my brother Freddie, my sister Anna, my sister Roma, my sister Mary were all arrested for guns, uh, drug sales, robberies. They have all been in prison.

My father used alcohol and my brother shot heroin, and my sisters drank—my mother used to sell reefer. My sister Doris was hospitalized for a nervous breakdown.

My family used violence all of the time. My parents threw things at each other, pushed, shoved, slapped, kicked, and punched each other. They definitely beat each other. They even used weapons against each other. My mother to my father, my father to my mother. They used whips and a knife called a machete. Uh, and those little baseball bats. They're real small. They did all of these things to me too. My mother had these slippers that, uh, has nails stuck inside of them. And, uh, she had kicked back at me because I didn't sweep the bedroom. And the nails got stuck. I have a mark to this day on my leg.

My father sexually abused me. It first started when I was 9, and he kept doing it. My mother knew.

By the time I was 9, I was in and out of foster homes because my father was physically abusing me. I never checked in with any of my foster parents about where I was going or what I was doing. I left when I was 15 because I was emancipated. I also lived in a group home where I got jumped by the other girls.

When I was 13, I was put in a mental hospital for unstable behavior. I was hitting myself, fighting. I mean I was just fighting all over the place. I actually did things to hurt myself. I tried to end it all by trying suicide.

Monica's view of her family, again, was typical of other women in our study. By and large, they viewed their parents as unable to love or be nurturing. Often, their parents' inadequacies were due to their own personal difficulties, including alcohol and drug abuse, unemployment, and mental health problems. Further, many of the women were exposed, as children, not only to their parents' illegal use of drugs, but also to parental involvement in drug distribution. Here is Denise's description of her family:

My mother and father were married. But he came and goes as he pleased. He was there a while, he was gone a while. But they basically stayed married. My mother was an alcoholic—Valium taken behind the counter, shit. Valiums was my thing too. I got them everyday, them and a joint and wine and anything else was Kool and Gang. It was all in my mother's house.

My father was a laborer and he was also a drug dealer. Pretty busy guy. I found out one day at like a family dinner—a few of his friends, his colleagues. I asked him for like $100 and he said no, and I was furious. His friends said, you're not toasting your father? And I said no. And he said, why not? And I said, which career am I toasting? The one in the daytime, or the one at night? That's all I said to him and he said go to your room. I said all right. I got upstairs, he flipped, I flipped, and I said I know what you do. I know how you pay for this shit. I know every fuckin' thing about you 'cause I'm out there. You fuckin' sell heroin, you sell crack, you sell dope, you sell wine, you sell every mother fuckin' thing. The only difference between you and Carlos and all of them is that they fuckin' stand on the corner and be real and you stand behind them and pull the fuckin' strings. He whipped my ass real good after this. His way of standing up to you was slapping you from here to there. But no matter how bad I was hurt, we could never go to the doctor because we couldn't let the neighbors know that.

But I used to stick up my fathers' workers. And then he hired me to sell coke and dope. But, I was put in the Children's Shelter for vandalism and just some other shit.

My uncle lived with us, too. He was like a constant felon. He was constantly in jail all the time for something—either it was stealin' on down to robbery back up to boosting and back down again. He taught me how to boost. He was an IV drug user. My uncle use to whip my ass. My father used to whup my ass and yell. My mother would try. My grandmother hit me, but she didn't mean it. They used cords, belts, extension cords, sticks, anything that they could get their hands on. Especially my uncle. He'd use anything he could get his hands on because he knew that if I got up, I was comin' at him too. After a while, ass whippin' was just not the move anymore.

My father would curse my mother out. He would go upside her head. She would go upside his head. My uncle would beat up his wife. My grandmother was like, she would like just sit there like me and just chill. She went fuck it. I saw my uncle go raise his hand with a bottle to my grandmother. And as he did it, I pulled out my pistol and I, boom, I shot the bottle out his hand. And I told him don't do that. That's my girl. Do not fuck with her. Ya'll can fuck with each other, and kill each other, but don't fuck with her.

I was hospitalized, once. I had a terrible habit of like smashin' me against things. When I was angry, I would throw, break things, and do it with my hands. They put me on a antidepressant but I can't remember the name of it.

I felt my family didn't care. They didn't care. Sometimes my mom would ask where I was going. I'd say out, Mom. My grandmother would be the one to stand up to me. She would say you're doing this wrong. She found my razor and my pistol. She would take 'em. But I would tell my grandma that there's not really much you could do. I think my family needed to give a damn. I think they didn't need to be what they were. Now, I think they were like stupid.

Jackie's family, too, were perceived as not being there for her:

I lived with both of my parents, but I wouldn't say they raised me. I wouldn't say it was stable. It was a lot of violence at home. Constant violence. My parents beat each other and they beat me. My parents were frustrated. Often they used an extension cord to beat me. Once my father sexually abused me. When I was 5 the building super sexually molested me and once a babysitter did. Another time it was my uncles, you know, who frequently had hand problems. They touched all the time, and they drank, and they felt and they touched.

My parents weren't there for me.

Although these women perceived their parents as being instrumentally and expressively absent, for many "street parents" (Anderson, 1994), the frustrations and lack of hope that are concomitant with persistent poverty contributed to the time bomb that ticked within the family unit. As parents responded to even the slightest irritations with violence, the children were taught a lesson. "They learn that to solve any kind of interpersonal problem one must quickly resort to . . . violent behavior" (Anderson, 1994:83). Certainly, this was the case for Jocorn:

> My mother and father raised me. I had 11 brothers and sisters. Eight girls and the rest of them boys. My mother was a factory worker and my father a security guard. But to make ends meet, you know, they would like do money on the side.
>
> My father has been arrested. My brother has been picked up. Another brother went to jail for direct sales.
>
> My father had a drug problem, alcohol. And being that he was diabetic, I always told him that. But he didn't seem to care. I had another brother who did any kind of drug.
>
> There was a lot of violence in my house. My father pulled out a knife on my mother. My mother took the pot and knocked him out. My mother used to get fed up with him and ask him to leave. She had him arrested, too. One time, my sister was crying and he had wanted her to shut up, you know. He threw a cup at her, you know. He told me not to react. But, yeah, I reacted. There was a time, I was brewing coffee and I threw it on him cause this is like a 7-year-old kid and he threw a cup at her because she's crying and she's hungry, you know, and stuff like that. And, you know, I was like where are you at?
>
> Then he had these days when he smoked—like 100 percent proof liquor. He was a maniac.

The family's failure to perform their "guardian functions" (Sampson and Groves, 1989) and to socialize their children in terms of decency (Anderson, 1994) is clear from the preceding accounts. In addition, their inabilities were compromised even further by a strong mandate requiring that all personal matters, especially troubles, be kept to themselves. Thus, despite the lack of consideration they show family and community members, "street parents" have a superficial concern that others view them as in control, especially of their children and their children's immediate environment. Therefore, when confronted with troubles, traumas, tragedies, upsets, disappointments, and victimizations, the women in our study were left to their own inner resources to cope. Under the best of circumstances, given their lives, the likelihood of dealing effectively with the types of problems these women confronted was not good.

These families, incapable of providing protection and guidance, also deprived the women of support that could have been given by members of their larger networks. Thus, the women were denied the benefits of guardianship but also those of "social resources" (Oliver, 1995) that may have helped them cope with their problems. L.G. shared with us her feelings of isolation. Despite the fact that her family was "intact," their own problems with employment, alcohol, and drugs militated against their protecting and supporting L.G., especially after her rape. As she talks about her feelings of guilt and loneliness after the rape, she places it in the context of her family structure:

> Uh, my stepfather was an alcoholic, and my mother was a welfare recipient. In my family, one of the things my mother would always talk about to us is what goes on in the house stays in the house. And so I didn't have no way of ventilatin' or expressin' how I felt about what was going on at home; and my stepfather, who was an alcoholic, fought and beat on my mother. He would pull a knife on her. But she would take the knife from him and pull it on him. He would fight her and not give her money. And she was very dependent on him. I have a brother, too. When I was growing up, he was arrested for possession and sale. He's a drug user. Crack, dope, whatever. He's a garbage head. He's the one who turned me on to crack.
>
> My mother, though, she was one of those women who would let you hang yourself, you know, give you enough rope to hang yourself. Even when I was raped, I didn't go to her about it. I never told anybody about it. I never reported it. I think in the back of my mind that I had it coming to me. I had no one to tell me different. I couldn't tell anybody.
>
> You know, to go out and do the things I did was influential ... I mean influenced because I didn't have the family structure and help when I was growing up. So, a lot of the things I did, I knew were wrong.

Stephanie too described a family life bereft of support and bonds to conventional institutions. Her estrangement from positive social resources, like the school, eventually led her to a Harlem street gang and away from junior high school.

My mother and father were alcoholics. They was always drinkin'. My parents used to push and shove and beat each other. My dad knifed her in her mouth one time. He molested me and my sister. My mom used to beat me with an extension cord. She also used a curtain rod. I had whelps, I had bruises on my legs and stuff. I missed a lot of school. She kept me home from school so that no one knew about this stuff.

My sister and brother were crackheads. At 11 or 12, my mom started lettin' us drink. She didn't really try to make us go to school. By 15, this all seemed okay, and I did and went what I wanted.

For the women with whom we spoke, the realities of life in "street families" were exacerbated by their marginalization from larger prosocial and guardian networks. Unlike earlier eras of inner-city family life, in the period we have explored, the women did not have positive extended-family relationships, involvement with a caring "old head" (Anderson, 1994:86), or church affiliations, and they did not attend settlement or after-school programs. Further, as we will now see, they were estranged from school, as well.

Life in School

Generally, the research on childhood experiences in the confines of the school posits, at best, a weak or indirect relationship with delinquency or violent offending (Fagan, Piper, and Moore, 1986; Jarjoura, 1993; LaGrange and White, 1985). Furthermore, studies of the effect of dropping out of school on criminal involvement, too, are equivocal in terms of strength and direction of the association. There are some studies that indicate that dropping out has no direct effect on criminal involvement (Bachman et al., 1978; Chavez et al., 1989; Jarjoura, 1993) or that it actually reduces involvement (Elliott and Voss, 1974) or that it actually increases delinquent behavior (Thornberry et al., 1985).

Our conversations with the women in our study failed to shed light on the direction or strength of these arguments. None of the women accounted for their involvement in street crime by stating that the conditions in school, such as boredom, discipline, or poor performance, caused them to cut class, drop out, or commit crimes to counter negative school experiences.

Nonetheless, during our discussions, it became clear that the school did provide a context in which larger processes were played out. Principally, there appeared to be the normal types of adolescent issues that were being performed in school. It is during adolescence that girls undergo a series of biological and social changes that require serious adjustments. And it is during this time that girls act in ways to define themselves apart from their families of origin, are most vulnerable to peer pressure, and, ironically, are most in need of familial support. Even among the most stable girls, involvement in a variety of deviant behaviors is part of the *normal* adjustment processes (Pipher, 1994; Caspi et al., n.d.; Stattin and Magnusson, 1990).

The school has been considered by some to be an important context in which girls test out their responses to changes (Caspi et al., n.d.). It is the social context in which opportunities for social interaction, self-evaluation, and bonding occur. Further, it is one of the places where "youth who emerge from street oriented families . . . develop a decency orientation" (Anderson, 1994:86). However, it is also within the school context that deviant activities receive the greatest support, specifically by peers, not only in terms of initiation, but in terms of maintenance, too (Caspi et al., n.d.).

It was in the school environment that many of these women met their delinquent peers. And it was with these peers that these women engaged in truancy, vandalism, fighting, drug experimentation, and other misbehaviors. Although we save our discussion of peer effects on violent offending for the next chapter, we believe a discussion of school experiences will set the stage for understanding what it was these women were doing while the rest of us were sitting in classes.

What were these women doing? Sixty-seven percent of the women reported that by the age of 10, they were involved, regularly, in fights on school premises. By the age of 13, 89 percent were regularly truant, 26 percent regularly carried weapons with them to school, and 15 percent were involved in school vandalism. Further, it should be noted that the majority of the women in our study, 75 percent of them, dropped out before completing high school. In many ways, their disengagement from school was part of a larger process in which social bonds to various conventional institutions were being eroded. As the women decreased school attendance, the opportunities for positive socialization were attenuated. However, from their accounts, a pattern of deviant and criminal behaviors was well established before their leaving school. Here, Denise recounts her schooldays:

> I used to get into fights every day. It must have started when I was 7. And my mother was called every day. We used to fight about anything—from you called me a name to I didn't like the way you looked. I'd fight with both boys and girls—it didn't make a difference. I didn't discriminate. You pushed me, I pushed you back.
>
> I started cutting classes, drinking, and doing coke and reefer when I was about 13 or 14, in seventh grade. We used to blow up our lockers and other peoples lockers that we disliked. We used to do this for kicks.
>
> My friends were basically into the same things as I was. We used to cut classes and burglarize people's houses, we would destroy shit, we would go to the park—a group of us, five or six girls, we used to stick up couples. We'd grab the girlfriend, I'd hold the razor. Guys are like apt to give you like whatever so you won't hurt his girl.
>
> By tenth grade this seemed more exciting, and some of my other friends were dropping out, so I left to hang with them.

L.G. also dropped out of school to hang with her friends:

> One of the reasons I dropped out was, uh, hangin' out with the crowd and, you know, wantin' to be part of, um . . . just, you know, just a lot of wantin' to hang out with everybody else and cutting a lot of tenth grade. We were experiencing drinkin' beer and, you know, things like that. Smokin' marijuana . . . we were doing things like that. And we'd fight. Girls went to scratch up each other's face and stuff like that.
>
> I used to get into a lot of fights at school. Started when I was around 11. I was like a school bully, you know. At first, I was one of those kids in public school who wouldn't fight back. And, you know, being a house of only two children, just my brother and I—he taught me to fight and, you know, I became very popular in school because I would fight back. You know, a lot of the children would look up to me and, you know, I was like the leader. You know, and I was a bully and, you know, I took advantage of people who wouldn't fight back that were just like myself at one time.
>
> We also did a lot of graffiti. Started when I was 13. A lot of my activities were when I was 13. A lot of it stemmed from my home. You know, uh, a lot of the things that a lot of the other children had cause they had mothers and fathers who worked, uh, I didn't have. And, you know, wantin' a lot of nice things and wantin' to be part of the

crowd, uh, drinkin' beers and bein' the bully allowed me to be part of it without having all the materialistic things that the other children had.

And then, by tenth grade, mostly all of us were dropping out of school.

In school, children act out their life experiences in interaction with others. Having witnessed aggression and violence in the home and realizing that the winner was always the one with greater physical skill, these women gained respect and self-esteem by practicing what they learned at home: "Might makes right, and toughness is a virtue, while humility is not" (Anderson, 1994:86).

Jocorn, too, dropped out in tenth grade, but not until after she had established a career of fighting and street crime.

Yeah, I was a little involved in school, but I guess due to the fact that there's always arguments in the house with family members, and in the neighborhood I grew up in too, school wasn't so important. Basically, what I seen in my family and neighborhood is what I thought was okay, and that was what I was taught—so who needed school? I figured, since I saw it at home and on the streets that gettin' high was okay. But in school, I had a lot of problems.

I was 9 when I first started fighting in school. With teachers, security guards. I was always short, and I was always being bullied around. I didn't like being bullied around. So I used to carry knives. One girl, I had a fight with 32 times. I counted them all. She came at me with a razor blade, right. She didn't like me. She was jealous of me, like, I had a lot of attention from the guys and stuff like that. She was like a bully at school, too. And I had like a blade in my pocket. I wasn't sure what she was goin' to do. I just took it out and I felt somebody behind me, so I just, I was scared, and I went and nipped her in the neck.

By the time I was 12, I was drinking and smoking reefer at school. I also did a lot of graffiti. My school friends were basically involved in drugs and burglaries. I was doing all of this to be a part of it, you know. I wanted to be accepted, to be part of a crowd. I wanted to be down with the friends, like they say.

Janelle dropped out of school in eleventh grade:

Basically, you know, my friends . . . all of us played hooky. I wanted to be negative. I had a negative boyfriend, too. I started fighting, though, in elementary. I fought every day. I wasn't getting enough attention at home. I would pull girls' hair, take their things, you know, like money, or, you know, like little keys, rings. You know how little girls come to school with little things to play with. I used to take them. And when they'd find out, we'd fight. When I was 13, I started carrying razors with me to school. I was also doing a lot of drugs at that time. I'd used the razors sometimes when I was paranoid when I was high.

Alicia drifted in and out of school until she finally left in eleventh grade.

You know, my mother used to drink a lot. I started drinking in school in seventh grade. I was always in classes for troubled kids. I used to fight a lot. I was a very violent kid. I used to beat my sister, and my mother was always beating me with an extension cord. So, I just started taking it out on the kids at school. I used to beat up the girls and take their money. I was wild in school. I started fighting in fourth grade and began carrying weapons when I was 15. I also started smokin' reefer then too. Living in Brooklyn and having a bad home life were two tough things to bring to school. I had a bad girl reputation at school. And I had a couple of girlfriends in school who used to steal lunch money with me to get attention. Then, we started cuttin' school and robbin' people in the streets. That was also about the same time my stepfather used to molest me. My mother knew, but she was scared of him. He used to beat the hell out of her. You know, it was the environment. My mother was always calling me stupid, dodo bird. And so, I thought that I was stupid. So I finally left school in eleventh grade.

By the time these girls were adolescents, they had either internalized the normative orientations found in their homes and replicated in the schools, or they had at least decided that it was necessary to behave as if they did. These street orientations centered on presenting oneself as capable of taking care of business, of not needing anyone, of commanding respect. And these street orientations filled the daily lives of the women while they were still attending school. But these women also recognized the precariousness of their positions and so were constantly on the lookout for threats to their reputations. Stealing others' possessions, winning a fight, and perceiving each and every interaction as a potential threat to one's self-respect and reputation circumscribed their school experiences. During our conversations about school, the women never spoke about the curriculum, their teachers, the administration, or classroom interactions. Instead, their descriptions of school days revealed their almost exclusive concern with finding their place in street life.

Distress During Adolescence

The early stage of adolescence is fraught with many ambiguities that are caused by biological, dispositional, and contextual changes (Pipher, 1994; Caspi et al., n.d.). Beginning with adolescence, youth *normally* move from attachments to family to attachments to peers; it is when they *normally* experiment with drugs, alcohol, and sexuality; it is when they are *normally* most vulnerable to social labeling; and it is also when they are *normally* more in need of careful yet subtle support from their families and other neighborhood social institutions (Pipher, 1994).

Most of us can remember how, when we reached adolescence, our parents became openly concerned about the type of people who were our friends. Never before had they expressed such "interest" in our friends' grades, hobbies, interests, and other activities. Never before did they query us on how our friends felt about various situations. When confronted with an activity that our parents found problematic, they made their war cry the old rant and rave: "So, if your friends jumped off the Brooklyn Bridge (we both grew up in New York City), would you?" (Okay, we admit to asking our own daughter, who is now in early adolescence, if she would jump off the roof of the Beverly Center Mall if her friends did.)

But these parental worries, including our own, are not so far off from the concerns of contemporary criminologists. A substantial body of research has suggested that the more delinquent friends one has during adolescence, the more likely one is to become delinquent oneself (Agnew, 1991; Akers et al., 1979; Elliott et al., 1985; Tittle et al., 1986; Warr and Stafford, 1991).

The initiation and timing of entry into offending careers are key developmental life events and play a critical role in future social outcomes. Although the life course is dynamic in that developmental courses can be waylaid or rerouted, much research points to the importance of certain developmental issues, especially during early adolescence, that move children from having "conduct problems" to being initiated into criminality (White, 1992; Zucker, 1991).

Although it has been well established that peers play a critical role in the production of offending behavior, this research has been limited to understanding *male* initiation. A significant part of the literature on women and crime contends that women are "forced" into offending by males, drug addiction, victimization histories, and the responsibilities of single parenthood (Arnold, 1990; Huling, 1991; Miller, 1986; Pollack-Byrne, 1990; Weisheit and Mahan, 1988). By and large, it is argued that domestic arrangements provide two important conduits through which women enter into criminal careers.

When offending begins early in a woman's life, childhood victimization is viewed as the main cause of female offending. Since between 50 percent and 80 percent of women surveyed in various correctional institutions in the country reported being victims of domestic violence (Bureau of Justice, 1991), a direct, causal relationship is posited between "the experience of being victimized and subsequent offending" (Arnold, 1990). The chain of events leading to criminalization is then typically stated as beginning with child physical or sexual abuse, which produces a vicious cycle that includes running away, institutionalization, return to dysfunctional family unit, running away, and ultimately street deviance (e.g., prostitution, drug use).

When initiation into offending occurs later in a woman's life, single parenthood is seen as another family-based pathway into offending. Given data documenting the large proportion of women offenders who are also mothers of young children, it is argued that women are driven into criminal activities by the responsibilities of single parenthood thrust upon them by the desertion of an uncaring and often abusive male partner (Douthat, 1988; Glick and Neto, 1977; Moss, 1986; Roman, 1990).

When pathways to violent crime are not found in the home environment, some criminologists have argued that drug use itself leads women into criminal careers (Arnold, 1990; Huling, 1991). The argument is that heavy involvement with drugs reduces the options for women to engage in other income-producing endeavors. Therefore, illegal activities provide women with opportunities to make enough money to buy drugs.

Notable for its absence in the literature on women's initiation into crime, however, is the possibility that initiation into offending, especially street violence,[2] may in fact be linked to the same sets of processes as for males, especially in terms of the role that *peers* play in this dynamic. This prospect remains unexplored or is openly rejected (Daly and Chesney-Lind, 1988). Instead, women's introduction to street crime continues to be viewed in isolation from the larger context in which these women grow up and in which they struggle through adolescence, a normally difficult phase of the life course. Here, we explore the taboo topic of female adolescents actually *choosing* to become involved with delinquent peers, who, by the way, are almost always females and who engage in violent street crime, as well.

Initiation into Violent Offending During Adolescence

Approximately 60 percent of the women in our study reported initiation into violent offending during the earlier stage of adolescence, that is, between the ages of 11 and 15. These women routinely engaged in violent physical confrontations with schoolmates, other peers, strangers, and family members, often using a weapon. They reported routinely cutting out of school to have "hooky parties." And it was during these parties that these girls engaged in a range of behaviors that included shoplifting, burglaries, robberies, and *later*, drug experimentation. Frequently, this was followed by initiation into the drug trade as street sellers.

By early adolescence, these early-onset women had already been labeled as "negative" or "troubled" by school administrators. They exhibited a wide range of problem behaviors, consistent with what has been called "problem behavior syndrome in adolescence" (Jessor and Jessor, 1977). Some had been removed from the general student population and placed in special classes. Others officially remained on the school attendance rolls but rarely attended classes.

These early-onset girls had, since elementary school, associated with peers who also engaged in problem behaviors. But for these girls, peers seemed less to *influence* their behavior than to reinforce earlier patterns that were established in interaction with family members, usually brothers, sisters, or cousins. This does not come as a total surprise; recently, there has been a growing body of research that has explored the role that siblings (and extended family members such as cousins) play in influencing the development of deviant conduct (Rowe and Gulley, 1992). This may be due to several factors: (1) The lifestyles of siblings may create opportunities for deviant involvement (Rowe and Gulley, 1992); (2) emotional attachment between siblings may produce greater behavioral resemblance—a greater willingness to model behavior after each other (Rowe and Gulley, 1992); or (3) sibling conflict may produce more generalized patterns of aggressivity (Patterson, 1984, cited in Rowe and Gulley, 1992).

Here, Monica tells us of her family's influence:

Oh, yeah, my two brothers and six sisters all were very close. They were older than me. When I was a little kid, my brother Victor and brother Freddie, along with my sister Anna and my sister Roma and my sister Mary, were all into robberies, guns, and later drug sales. My father was an alcoholic, my brother shot heroin, my mother sold reefer. My sister Doris was the only one not into it. She had a nervous breakdown. I used to love to hang out with them. They were always talking about how exciting their stuff was and sometimes, especially when I got to be about 10 or 11, they would let me come along with them.

Then, when I got older, maybe 12 or 13, I went out on my own with my friends. I hung with people who had talents. We'd make a little bomb kind of like thing and put them in police officer's cars like the little cars that looked like mail trucks. And we'd drink and sometimes meet my brothers and sisters and hang with them.

Oh, yeah, around that time, we started smokin' reefer—me and my girlfriends. They would just pass the joint around and I'd take. I just took it. Then when I was about 14, I was hangin' out with a crowd that smoked angel dust. At 15 I started gettin' into ludes [methaqualone], but just on weekends. These were things we just did on the side—sort of to party.

In Monica's case, as with many of the others in the early-onset group, sibling (in some other cases, cousin) effects on her deviant behavior preceded, and were then reinforced by, her involvement with delinquent peers. This familial resemblance may be due to the influence of a "moderator" factor (Baron and Kenny, 1986, cited in Rowe and Gulley, 1992), such as neighborhood or family distress that preconditions these behaviors, rendering these women "deviance-prone" (Zucker, 1991).

On the other hand, 40 percent of the women we interviewed had no early history of antisocial conduct. They were not involved in violent street behavior until the latter years of adolescence, from age 15 on. Take the case of Stacie, for instance:

> Until I was 15, I was really involved in school. My brothers and I were in the Boys Club. That was a real positive thing. From the Boys Club we got involved in a lot of activities. We got into swimming, and, uh, we got into a lot of little talent things. We did some, uh, traveling with the Boys Club for tournaments and Ruckers, you know, we went to shows and things. It was really good for my brothers and me.
>
> Until then, I was doing really well in school. My brothers and I weren't violent when we were young. Sometimes, though, I fought with boys when they pulled my hair and made fun of certain things. But I didn't really get into fighting until I was 15.
>
> Everything started when I was about 15. The kids I was hangin' with outside of school were a pretty wild crowd. It was great. I could get really loose with them. We'd smoke marijuana, cut out of school, write our names on walls—we wanted to be out there. We'd fight other groups of kids.
>
> At the beginning, I led a double life. I was doing really well in school. My friends in school were all "A" students and into sports. And when I was home, I cleaned the house and helped my brothers and sisters with their homework. When I was home and when I was in school, I just did everything positive. When I was with my friends outside of school, I did everything negative. I was really attracted to negativity. Then I started hangin' with them more because the attraction was so strong. They had pistols and knives and they got into mugging. I guess this part of the thrill of being there—the fact that there was an element of danger. I liked it. I liked it. It was part of the fun. Then we all got into LSD, angel dust, powdered cocaine, and stuff. That was when I was about 16. We would drink and get high and then go to the park. I would do anything they wanted to do. I wanted to be accepted by them, they were fun. They didn't make me go out mugging with them, but I wanted to. It wasn't really peer pressure, but there was a feeling that I had to do it if I really wanted to be accepted.

For later onset girls like Stacey, peers played a more direct role in their initiation into violent street offending. Furthermore, unlike the early-onset group, drugs were much more central to their interactions. For this later onset group, initiation occurred because of situational pressure to jointly participate in what was primarily a social behavior.

The transition from "positive" peer interactions to ones that were "negative" did not appear to be drastic. The gradual replacement of prosocial peers with delinquent ones occurred over a 1- to 2-year period of time, during the middle stages of adolescence. For that matter, the women in the later onset group recalled holding on to their prosocial friends for quite a while before leaving them to join their delinquent peers full-time; sometimes, though, their positive peers began to shun them. As April recounts:

I used to have two groups of friends. One group, the positive one, I had been in since elementary school. The other group was always getting into trouble. I began to hang with this crowd when I was 15— to fit in. And I began to like it because it made me feel like I was important. My friends who were always doing everything right tried telling me, uh, what I'm doing, I'm doing wrong and stuff like that. Some of them shied away from me a bit. As time went on, I let go.

I started drinkin' when I was 15 and I was doin' it regularly. And when I would meet people they would lead me to the progression of the drugs and that's what I did. My first crowd was into drinking and smoking pot. And then I met another crowd that was into cocaine. Both groups were all girls. I did that for a while and I kin' of grew out of that. Then a girl friend introduced me to crack. I liked that a lot better. I didn't like to be drunk so I didn't really like alcohol. I didn't like reefer because I felt I couldn't function. I didn't like cocaine because of the way it affected my nose, my nostrils. And the crack seemed like, you know, it felt like it made me more alert.

For Stephanie, the pathway was quite similar:

Everything really started when I was 15. I was actually doing okay in school. But at that age, I had, I don't know, I had a need to be with friends and let go. My friends were all from school. I had two groups of friends that I worked with. One was positive and the other was negative.

My positive friends knew I was hanging with the others, but it really didn't matter to them. Sometimes they would say you better not go there. Like when it was coming down to playing hooky, it was like either go to school with this group or play hooky wit' the other. When I would play hooky, they would help me out by giving me the things I missed in school and the homework.

When I was hanging out with the others, we was doin' shoplifting, drinking wine, and smokin' marijuana. The shopliftin' was for the excitement that became in the blood after a while. You know, I really got high off of getting over in stores and things; and many times I had plenty of money in my pocket and I would still go and steal things. I got a lot of attention from these friends, from my shopliftin'. Even though it was negative attention. We then got into burglaries and robberies. That was when I was about 16.

My parents didn't know about my runnin' around. I lied, I kept secrets. They only knew my positive friends. When they found out about the others and tried to keep me in the house, I was defiant. I stayed out. They gave up.

For the women in the later onset group, peer initiation into violent street offending brought with it a change in how they interacted with their parents. They reported an increase in lying to their parents about their out-of-school whereabouts and in sneaking out of their parents' apartments in order to join friends. At precisely the point when these girls needed parental supervision and support in order to overcome the pull toward street life, the parents gave up. Some parents locked their daughters out of the house after curfew, others heightened their physical responses, and yet other parents sent their daughters away—to live in foster care, to live with a neighbor, or to a psychiatric hospital. In all of these cases, the types and levels of parental supervision of their daughters' behaviors changed, and like their male counterparts, these girls began to spend more time away from home, in unstructured activities with peers, and becoming more heavily involved in street life.

Regardless of whether the woman was in the earlier or later onset group, by the age of 16 or 17 the overwhelming majority of these girls had dropped out of school, permanently. Their relative independence from parental and school controls gave way to the importance of their peers as direct influences on violent street offending. And given the neighborhood context, the opportunities for such activities were abundant.

Unlike other adolescents, though, these women's involvement in problematic and experimental behaviors did not recede in late adolescence. For that matter, by their accounts, their involvement in violent street offending, drug use, and other antisocial conduct *increased* as they entered young adulthood. This may be accounted for, partly, by both quantitative and qualitative changes in their drug use.

The Special Role Played by Drugs

Research on adolescent problem behavior syndrome (Elliott et al., 1989; Jessor and Jessor et al., 1977; Osgood et al., 1988; Robbins et al., 1962; White, 1992; Zucker, 1991) has pointed to the salience of drug use patterns in explaining the persistence of problem behaviors into adulthood. Unfortunately for us, this literature relies almost exclusively on general population samples in which the base rates of involvement in violent offending are low and the concentration of effects of impoverishment cannot be distinguished. These parameters further impede an understanding of the persistence of problem behaviors for *females*, for whom base rates are even lower. Nonetheless, the focus on drug use as a bridge between adolescent and young adult problem behavior is especially appropriate for the women with whom we spoke. For it was an increasing engulfment in drugs that seemed to "tip" the scales from experimentation and *social* uses to addiction and commitment to violent street offending.

For the early-onset group, drug abuse did not cause the onset of violent behavior. As we saw from prior accounts, the women in our study reported long and significant "careers" in violence that preceded drug use. The early-onset women were involved in fighting, burglaries, and robberies for two or more years before they turned to drugs. And their turn to drugs appeared to be correlated more with their deeper entrenchment in the roles associated with street life than with the adolescent social use of drugs.

Drug use for the early-onset group expanded their repertoire of street activities. It increased their contact with entrenched members of local drug markets—users and sellers—and it expanded their opportunities to participate in both these roles. Until the point of addiction, though, drug use for this group remained ancillary to their involvement in a more generalized lifestyle on the street that included a wide variety of criminal activities of which violence was a big part. However, once addicted, drugs played an important role in amplifying the involvement of these women in violent street crime, to a large extent in order to support drug *habits*. This was the case for Alicia:

> We'd been together since we were 12. We'd be stealin' from other kids—a couple of girlfriends of mine and me. I just wanted to be a

part of it. We used to buy cigarettes, beers, you know. And that's when Boone's Farm was out. But it was the fun of robbin' that was what got us.

And then it progressed. When I was 15, I started payin' more attention to robbin' people in the streets, you know, not just other kids. I liked it. It was really exciting. I started takin' blotter, drinking a bit more. I liked the high life. I liked hangin' out with my friends and everything. I liked the robbin'.

By the time I was 16 or so, I wanted to get down and sellin' seemed one way. I started hangin' more with the people who sold us drugs. First, I started selling opium, then reefer. Then around 17, I started selling dope in Bushwick, my neighborhood. After a while, though, I was bringin' in $800 a week just from dealing. I still did some robbin' with my friends—just for old times. Then, we'd buy some stuff, sit around and get high. Then, I got into freebasin'. I started gettin' into the life. By 17, I was hangin' out all night, freebasin' and selling, sleepin' all day. I got into the night life. But, I couldn't make it just from selling. So I went back to robbin' and found some friends to do burglary. The more I got into those drugs, the more I had to sell and rob.

For the later onset group, the pattern of initiation into violent street offending was different. Here, there was a clearer drug-crime connection. Gazella's story was typical:

I was doin' real well in school. I was on honor roll. I was on the gymnastics team; I was a cheerleader and in the drama club. Then, when I turned 16, this all ended. Things really changed. My friends got into drugs and wine. They also did some shoplifting. And I wanted to be with them. They started associating with people that were like, they had like criminal records, juvenile delinquency, you know. They were already on drugs. You know, they were already addicted. It was new to me and that's the path that I led. They would bring drugs around, and I was curious and I wanted to find out.

I started getting into fights when I was high. Got to a point that I began carrying a knife to school. That was when I was 16. The only people I looked up to at that time were the people in the high life. I'm sure there were good people out there, but I couldn't see them. By the time I was 17, I couldn't see much because of my drug use.

I started selling drugs in school. I sold pot. The pot belonged to a girlfriend of mine. I just wanted to make a couple of extra dollars. So she would give me half of her pot. One day the school found marijuana in my locker and they suspended me. That was eleventh grade; I never went back.

Upon leaving school, Gazella, like several of the other women in the later onset group, moved on to heroin and cocaine. The cost of increasing substance use was a major influence to engage in violent street offending, especially robbery and drug selling, in which the use of weapons is more common. And like the findings of other studies, our findings showed that these women's involvement in violent street crime quickly increased over the course of their addiction (Hayim, 1973; Nurco and DuPont, 1977; Voss and Stephens, 1973; Weismann et al., 1976).

Sheryl's initiation into violent street offending followed this pattern:

I was 16. I wanted to be a part of it, you know. I wanted to be accepted, to be part of a crowd. I wanted to be down with the friends, like they say. And they was into drugs and burglaries.

I first started with wine. Then with reefer, black beauties, acid, Valium. I was like the type—one drug after another. I'm a human garbage can, they call it. Within that first year, I had gone through so many drugs I started skinpoppin' too. Heroin was my drug of choice. I seen my friends doing it, you know, friends that I really liked a lot, you know. You know, I'd go, what is that. I thought it was a cigarette, but it wasn't. They told me to take a joint, and I started with a joint. It made me feel relaxed. I felt relaxed, you know. I felt like I was on a cloud. Heroin, I would go like in my own dream world and be relaxed. And I like cocaine because it made me feel excited.

I got into heroin when I went to a party where they have bowls all over the table. There used to be brown dope, you know. And white coke. But I got more into dope. I got real sick the first time, but then I started with a small amount and I didn't get greedy. The people I was hanging out with were really into drugs.

I started stealin' from my mother to buy drugs. My mother's a drunk, and I started stealin' from her. Then I started stealin' from other people, you know. My girlfriends—two of them—and I started robbin' people in the streets.

But it was coke that brought me to my knees, though. I was sniffin' cocaine at 17. You know, hangin' out with the big shots and everything. I thought it was cute. You know, hangin' out with them. And, you know, they got the money.

Thus, the "problem" behaviors of the women in our study did not recede when they reached young adulthood. Instead, the excitement, calm, and pleasure they experienced as a result of the pharmacological effects of their drugs, combined with their increasing marginalization from prosocial activities and deeper involvement with deviant peers, drove them further into street life.

Notes

1. These neighborhoods meet the criteria for "underclass" status regardless of whether the definitions are based on individual-level indicators of poverty (Jencks, 1991) or location-based aggregate measures (Jargowsky and Bane, 1990; Ricketts and Sawhill, 1988).

2. It should be noted here that those who operate within the dominant perspective in research on crime and female offending openly reject and militate against any discussion of female perpetration of street *violence*. They continue to force the discourse to remain within the parameters of "street deviance" (e.g., prostitution, drug addiction), and any reference to violent behavior is quickly quashed. Therefore, one continues to read the redundant studies of 20 women, selected purposively or conveniently, who are directed in their interviews toward supporting the dominant thesis of victimization.

Chapter Four

Work and Crime and Crime as Work

For most individuals, the key to a successful transition from adolescence to adulthood is finding a job. For many, this transition is facilitated by networks of kin and social and political contacts who assist in job placement. People who are in trade unions attempt to add their children and the children of family and friends to the rank and file; friends call other friends, colleagues, and others in their networks to help secure jobs for young people first entering the job market; and politicians place calls to government agencies and private employers in order to find jobs for the children of their constituents. Thus, informal social networks provide access for each succeeding generation to enter the labor market by providing information and personal contacts for young women and men to take advantage of job openings.

As we have discussed, the acute social distress in inner cities has disrupted these networks, both by the shrinking of manufacturing and public sector service jobs and by the changing composition of residents. As middle- and working-class minority families left neighborhoods for better living arrangements, they took with them the social capital of their complex relationships with younger members of the community, for whom they might have provided job information as well as role modeling and mentoring (Fagan, 1992). As a result, in neighborhoods such as the ones in which these women were raised and lived, most residents were neither working a traditional work week nor in traditional (licit) jobs, nor were they politically connected. Thus, the "disappearance of work" (Wilson, 1996), of social networks, and of mainstream aspirations and expectations vis-à-vis the workaday world textured the experiences of job hunting and job procurement for the women in our study.

Here, we describe how the women we interviewed tried to make a living. We explore their progression from early involvement in the legal and formal economy to their ultimate embeddedness in the informal and illicit economy. Through a description of their experiences in these various "work" sectors, the women provide us with an understanding of the bases for and types of decisions they made when choosing their "vocations." It is clear from their accounts that even from the outset, a tension always existed between their involvement in legal and illegal work and between the asocial world of formal labor and the seemingly social atmosphere promised by criminal involvement.

The Secondary Nature of
Secondary Labor Market Participation

For these women, employment was viewed as important, at least initially.[1] By the time they were 16, the majority had left school. Therefore, securing a job took on great significance. And at least at first, they were successful in finding employment. Most of them, 80 percent for that matter, were able to secure employment in the formal economy. These jobs were exclusively in the secondary labor market. Of the women who worked, the vast majority were employed in entry-level, unskilled positions as office clerks (32 percent), factory laborers (28 percent), and salespeople (25 percent). Fifteen percent of the women were able to obtain "aide" positions in home health care or education. These positions were acquired through either temporary employment agencies or public programs, never through personal networks. They lasted no more than a few months and were characteristically low paying, offering little long-term security and no chances for advancement.

For teens in less distressed neighborhoods, entry into the workforce through the secondary labor market has been considered the typical way in which to establish a work history. It was within this market that we started our resumes of job experiences. Here, we demonstrated perseverance, responsibility, self-discipline, and some skill development. Whether we were supermarket cashiers, department store clerks, or delivery boys (the latter position was literally held only by boys), we assumed that these situations were temporary yet somehow important for our futures. These experiences expanded our personal networks, helped pay for additional training or education, and showed the workaday world that we were on our way to more satisfying careers.

However, the women in our study entered the labor force with an acute awareness that their employment, even in the future, would in all probability be sporadic or remain in the lowest echelons of the secondary market. For the majority of the women, then, aspirations regarding employment were low. And for the few women who hoped for more lucrative futures in the licit job sector, training in cosmetology and having their own "station" at the local beauty salon was their loftiest goal. But even at the outset, these women were not going to be fooled into thinking that the jobs available to them would bring the "prestige, pride, and self-respect" (Liebow, 1967:60) found in white-collar occupations. Thus, like the men Liebow described in *Tally's Corner* (1967), these women ascribed "no lower value on the job than does the larger society" (p. 57). In other words, these women were keenly aware of the social value of the types of jobs available to them. As Liebow stated,

> neither the streetcorner man who performs these jobs nor the society which requires him to perform them assesses the job as one worth doing and worth doing well. Both employee and employer are contemptuous of the job. The employee shows his contempt by his reluctance to accept it or keep it, the employer by paying less than is required to support a family. Nor does the low wage job offer prestige, respect, interesting work, opportunity for learning or advancement, or any other type of compensation. (p. 56)

The work descriptions offered by the women we interviewed confirm this perspective. Furthermore, like the men Liebow described and those studied by Bourgois (1995), the women eventually came to view these jobs with an active disinterest. They were routinely fired due to excessive absenteeism or were absent frequently as a way of quitting. They would often show up for work high on drugs or coming down from a night of heavy drinking and partying. Often, especially toward the end of their involvement in the formal economy, they used their work environments as settings for their increasingly prevalent criminal activities.

Some might ask, why did these women engage in such self-defeating behaviors? Questions like this one have always plagued social researchers. Whether for Willis, in his study of working-class lads in England, or for Liebow (1967) or Anderson (1978) or Bourgois (1995), in their studies of urban street corner men, behaviors labeled by Wilson (1996) as "unflattering" and "ghetto related" are rooted in the particular combination of political, cultural, and economic forces that have been shaping inner-city neighborhoods since the 1960s. Whether residents of these neighborhoods work or not on any particular day or in any particular capacity is the result of a "complex phenomenon marking the intersection of economic forces, social values, and individual states of mind and body (Liebow, 1967:30).

Further exacerbating the situation is an orientation to the future that militates against commitment to the secondary labor market. Whereas residents in more stable communities view their initial employment in the secondary market as an investment in a future in which work will be economically and culturally rewarding, those in distressed neighborhoods view their futures as bleak and untouched by either the pecuniary or nonpecuniary advantages of employment. Thus, they concern themselves with satisfying their material and emotional needs whenever they have the opportunity to do. As Liebow discovered, "apparent present time concerns with consumption and indulgences—material and emotional—reflect a future time orientation. 'I want mine right now' is ultimately a cry of despair, a direct response to the future as he sees it" (Liebow, 1967:68).

Whether the ghetto poor can sustain employment in the licit world is shaped, as well, by the "cultural capital" they bring with them to the workplace (Bourgois, 1995:135). The same skills that bring them respect and success on the street make them seem incompetent, threatening, and lazy. Thus, the same behaviors that permit these women to walk through the social worlds of the street culture militate against their acceptance in the legal world.

The women we interviewed grew up in this context and within "street families," (Anderson, 1994) in which such behaviors and perspectives were prevalent. As a result, they too demonstrated the "disrespect and resistance" (Bourgois, 1995) and the "lethargy, disinterest and general apathy" (Liebow, 1967) that plague ghetto neighborhoods.[2] And consequently, these women lost their feelings of connectedness to work in the licit economy; they, like some of their neighbors, no longer "expected work to be a regular, and regulating, force in their lives" (Wilson, 1996:52).

It should be noted, though, that for the women in our study, some of the "unflattering behaviors" that prevail in inner-city neighborhoods were also developmental. The years between mid and late adolescence have been described by others as a period in which youth are normally more interested in their social lives than in establishing a work identity (Osterman, 1980; Sullivan, 1989:58). Thus, their commitment to the workaday world, especially one bereft of an active and vibrant social component, was at best tenuous.

Nonetheless, the tenuousness that might be defined as developmentally understandable, and certainly temporary, for youth in more functional communities is, in fact, more deleterious in distressed communities. Unfortunately, entering the formal economy during the mid to late teens has been found to overdetermine subsequent employment experiences for inner-city youth. The combination of typical adolescent behavior (including egocentrism, vulnerability to peer pressure, and risk taking) with the particular social and economic problems extant in distressed communities meant that, for these women, early failures in the labor market would have particularly disastrous consequences for subsequent employment (Freedman, 1969; Osterman, 1980; Sullivan, 1989) and for more general attitudes toward work.

Thus, as the women we interviewed floated from one job to the next, owing to the circumstances identified previously, rather than develop a resume of work experiences they demonstrated their inability to retain employment, obtain new job skills, or engage in activities that would launch their careers within the legal economy. Instead, these women became more deeply entrenched in criminal and deviant lifestyles; and it was *these* worlds the women we spoke to eventually turned to in an effort to make a living or just to "live."

The Initial Work Experience

When we listened carefully, for these women spoke "softly" about work, we were able to hear their frustrations over the limitations inherent in the secondary labor market. We needed to listen carefully also because these women had learned that to talk about work serves no purpose—a point to which we will return. We share the women's descriptions of how their involvement in crime or drugs further attenuated their bonds to the legal workaday world and finally brought about a rupture in those attachments. Herminia told us about her experiences in her first job (which were like all of the others):

> I worked for like minimum wage at Duane Reade Pharmacy. I enjoyed it cause, you know, I felt, like independent. I was bringing a little money home. But, fast I stopped liking it. I never liked a job that would be just standing like in one place, you know, like doing the same thing over and over. I got tired of it—the monotony, the routine everyday, so I stopped showing up. I lasted there about 4 months. Then, I worked in McDonald's for maybe 4 weeks. I hated McDonald's. It was boring. I was there for about 4 weeks. So, I went through a few other jobs. These were the only ones I could get. I had to lie about my age just to get these. I was only 15 and 16, and who was going to hire me?

Herminia's description was typical of the women in this study. Regardless of the actual position, like the men whom Liebow spoke with in *Tally's Corner*, all the women failed to display an "overt interest in job specifics . . . in a large part perhaps because the specifics are not especially relevant" (Liebow, 1967:57). This was due to the fact that the secondary job market was composed of "a narrow range of nondescript chores calling for nondescript, undifferentiated, unskilled labor" (Liebow, 1967:57). Thus, whether it was Herminia, Stephanie, or any of the other women, the descriptions of their initial employment situations were uniform in their recounting and in their content.[3] Stephanie monotonically told us:

> Well, when I started, I was working off and on in different cashiers and stuff like that. Started when I was 15. These were just menial jobs to me, and they really didn't matter. I never liked just sittin' down or standin' up types of jobs. But there was nothing else for me to do.

Janelle, too, describes her dissatisfaction with the types of jobs available to her. Furthermore, given her early involvement in violent street crime and drug use, it was especially difficult for her to accept the drudgery and routine of employment in the secondary market. Clearly, these types of jobs did not compete with the excitement she had and enjoyment she received from hanging out and partying with her friends.

> I used to work at—this was when I was 16—I used to work at Wendy's. Yeah, at Roy Rogers too. I worked like for 6 months at the first job and 2 months for the second. I quit because I couldn't function every day, gettin' up and goin' to work and then partyin' the night before. I didn't feel too great about these jobs. Wearing a stupid uniform and flipping burgers. That's lame.
>
> Yeah, I was trying to do something for myself by working these jobs. But it wasn't working. I rather go home and get high and hang out with my people. So, it wasn't workin' and neither was I.

It is interesting that even those who worked in the human service sector, principally as home attendants, viewed work similarly as demeaning, boring, and no different from clerical or sales work:

> I started out as a home health aide. It was okay for a little while. But then I got sick of it. You know what I'm saying—they like, they were driving me crazy. I felt like a housekeeper. It was nothing special, no different than working burgers or cleaning tables. There's not much else to say about it. (Denise)

Thus, the women in our study viewed their involvement in the licit job world with the same emptiness as the countless ghetto, barrio, and street corner residents studied by other researchers.

The Intermingling of Licit and Illicit Work

Initially, the women attempted to make a living, primarily through legitimate employment. Very quickly, however, they decided that the low economic and cultural returns from their marginal employment was not satisfactory, and they turned to crime and illegal hustles for supplementation. For many women, the workplace itself served as a setting for these activities. And it was these activities that provided them with important sources of income, identity, and excitement.

Here Denise, a former home attendant, describes how she combined licit and illicit work to augment her desires for more money, more excitement, and the respect of her peers on the street:

Yeah, so I hated doing things for these rich people, so after a while me and my friends developed a gimmick. I would go into the house, and I would case it out and get all the necessary information. When they would be out, my friends would come in and like vandalize it. They would come in and take all of the essential pieces. Then we'd all go out and party and celebrate our success. I was really a key connection for them. And, funny thing is, I would go back to work the next day like nothing ever happened and act shocked.

I did that for about 6 months. But I really couldn't stand cleaning up after these rich people and so I went to work at a hospital in their dietary department. Then I got the key to the supplies and I had my girlfriends come up with a truck and unload the block. This was fun and made us lots of money too. But I got arrested and had to give them my paycheck. I worked there for about 6 months too.

Monica, too, used her place of employment for her illegal enterprises. In this case, she dealt drugs from her office.

I started as a summer youth worker for a city agency. But then they kept me permanently as a floater, which means like I worked diversified duties. I worked with administration, receptionist, advertising— I did all of that. I made, like, $9,000 a year. At this point I was already indulging in cocaine, and I started selling drugs. So, uh, I started going to work and showing people my material—people that I knew that got high. And they started buying from me. So then they started buying weight, which would mean that I would have to get more material—and give it to them. And, uh, where, also it's like I used the messenger companies from the office. I used to call the messenger companies, and they used to pick everything up. And they would come pick it up at the agency and drop it off at someone else not knowing what was really inside. I made like $4000 to $5200 a week. It depends because I was still shopping for a lot of weight. I just wanted more money, and I just wanted to have my own—not work anymore—and travel. But then I just started using all the money for getting high and I stopped going to the office.

Crime on the Side

Other women recounted for us incredible work schedules in which, for the majority of the time they were employed in the legal sector, they would hold down "second jobs" during their off hours. The majority of these women were in the later onset group. Their over-riding addiction to drugs pushed them to secure money by any means possible, legal and otherwise. April was one such woman:

I was makin' like $7 an hour at this Sears job. That was actually pretty good money, but I was gettin' high. I was stealin', robbin', I used to forge checks to get more money. I worked there for maybe 6 months. I guess I was into fast money, a fast life. I needed money to support my habit. It was no way I could support my habit workin' on a job. So I needed money. So I went out, and, uh, the person that I was buying from, I asked him, you know, how can I get into it.

So, after I was done with my day at Sears, I was selling on the street. I turned out to be one of the carriers—the person that, uh, pick up the drugs and distribute it to people on the street to sell. I bring in about $2000–$3000 a week. Sometimes I, I would be up 2 or 3 days in a row because the money would be coming so fast that I'd be, I wouldn't want to go to sleep because I knew if I would go to sleep, I would miss money—the Sears money and the other—I wanted both.

Losing sleep, being absent from legal work, partying, and hustling also formed the day-to-day experience for some of the women in the early-onset group. For these women, crime on the side was a continuation of their long-term involvement in offending. Initially, it counterbalanced the asocial and boring nature of their jobs in the legal sector. It provided these women with the ex-citement, adventure, and camaraderie absent from jobs in the sec-ondary labor market. Further, and not unimportant, crime on the side supplemented the meager incomes they received from their marginal jobs.

L.G. recounts the following:

When I was like 15—when I dropped out of school after, you know, a lot of places weren't taking people that didn't have a high school diploma and stuff like that—I went to a temporary agency, you know, which allowed me to work for different companies. I did cleri-cal work for the Department of Probation. I did clerical work for AT&T and Citibank. I worked 6 or 7 months in each of these places. Usually the job itself had ended and I'd go back to the agency and they place me again. But they were all boring—no one to talk to, to hang out with, but I kept going. But even though I was workin' and still doin', you know, the right thing, I always was drawed to doin' the wrong thing somewhere down the line.

When I'd get home from work, I'd go hang out with my friends.
We got hooked up with some people who were, uh, transportin'
drugs from New York to New Jersey to Washington, and I started
doin' that for a while after work, on weekends, or between jobs. I
would get paid large sums of money and I, you know, I clung to that
for a while. But I was really into it for the fun and for things to do
with my friends. I did like the real money, though.

I did other stuff during this time, like stealin' in stores and rippin'
people off. Me and friends would go to parks and 34th and 42nd
Streets and stick people up. We got money, real money for clothes,
jewelry, and fun. But really soon getting the real money became the
important thing.

But then I got mixed up with harder drugs. I went further down
and stopped going to the temp agency. Smokin' crack was like, just
all I wanted to do. So, I sold crack for a percentage, just to have some
to smoke, I would sell. I would sell for drugs and collect welfare.

L.G., like many early-onset women, was socialized initially into
illegal behavior and violence for principally nonpecuniary reasons.
The money they received at that point in time was secondary to the
excitement and adventure they received from their participation.
However, as they entered their late teens and experienced a desire
for a more sustained income, L.G. and her early-onset peers ap-
plied the criminal "skills" learned earlier to economically motivated activities. But even within this context, noneconomic mo-
tives were important. For these women, committing crime with
friends and enjoying the fruits together were still meaningful.
Once addicted to harder drugs (i.e., crack cocaine), however, L.G.
and most of the women in this study experienced the ultimate rupture in ties to the licit workaday world and a decline in the importance of excitement, adventure, and peer participation in criminal
activities. Thus, by the time the women in this study reached
adulthood, whether they had been early or later onset, drug addiction and not peers organized most of their daily activities.

We should say that at this point in their lives, these women were
still successful in avoiding serious sanctions for their already
lengthy involvement in criminal activity. On the average, first arrests occurred when these women were in their early (for robberies) to mid twenties (for assault and drugs). Therefore, commitment to the illegal economy was viewed by these women as a
relatively low-risk endeavor.

Commitment to the Illegal Economy

Patterns of illegal work varied among the women. As we have mentioned, some abandoned work after periods of licit employment, whereas others drifted in and out of legal work while firmly committed to the illegal economy. Herminia's account was typical of this latter group of women:

> I had lots of little jobs, but selling cocaine was always how I really made my living. My last job was, I was 18, I was a receptionist at a showroom. I was there maybe 1 year. It was okay. But I was already into selling cocaine. I started that much earlier when my father went to jail. I knew my father was selling coke, but my father didn't know that I knew. I don't know for how long he was doin' it, and I realized that the money that was comin' into the house, into my mother's house, was coming from selling coke. And I felt that as my duty as taking care of my family I started selling coke. My father didn't know anything about it at first. But there came a time when we were doin' it together. We were selling together.
>
> Now, I'd be selling for about 7 years. I went up and down. I could make $500. I could make $3000 a week. It depended. I never stood on the corner and sold bags or anything like that. It would always be quantity. I had a few customers, four or five customers. I was selling ounces with some Colombians. They became like my suppliers and stuff. I started like with myself; when my father came out I started like working with him. Then I stopped working in offices altogether.

Alicia, too, considered her criminal activities as more important and more regular than her sporadic experiences within the legal economy:

> I had two jobs. I used to do factory work. I didn't like . . . it was too much labor, you know. You had to do everything. So I didn't like that. I did home attendant for a little while. It was okay. But, my main commitment was to doing robberies. After awhile doing both things, the home attendant thing and the robbery thing, I tried to slow down a bit. My mother had a stroke, and left me in custody of my brothers and sisters. So, I had to devote myself to one thing and I went back full time to robbing people.

Other women from the outset considered the illegal economy as their primary job commitment. They chose *exclusive* "careers" in crime and never participated in the secondary labor market. For these women, given the alternatives of low-wage payoffs from legal work and the expectation of relatively high returns from income-generating criminal activities, they viewed illegal work as a rational choice not unlike choices made among legitimate occupational pursuits (Fagan, 1994).

Jocorn and Rose, both early-onset, had a rich history of pre- and early-adolescent involvement in violence and crime. By the time they reached their mid teens, hustling was a way of life. As Rose recalls,

> like I said, I use to live in a neighborhood full of hustlers. And um, they use to watch me go to school, giving me $5 or $10 to buy clothes off the street for all the kids in the neighborhood. And then just, we started hanging down there by them. Then we started holding drugs for them. And paying us, $100 a day, and we would hold a hundred quarters, now if I would have gotten caught with that, lord knows how much time, but I was too naive and young to know what was going on. The money was good to me. I thought I was rich, you know what I am saying. And I liked to buy. So, by the time I left school, I was already into my job on the streets. I knew how to do the job, and I had no problem protecting myself while I was doing it.

Jocorn, too, was deeply entrenched in her "career" by the time she left school. And she stayed in this one job, advancing through the ranks until she had her own organization.

> I was about 11 or 12 when I started selling drugs. I'd sell reefer, Valiums, acid, syringes. It was fast money. I guess that's what attracted me to it, the fast money and the fun. I was makin' about $500 a week. Much later on, when I was about 17, I started like putting people to work for me. I was pulling in $10,000 a day. I'd moved to selling dope. I found with dope, like I had customers that would come from Boston to buy for $10 and sell them up there for $30. When I found this out, then I had people go out there and sell it. Then I got more money.
>
> I sold it all. Crack too. I've been dealing for 19 years. The more I had, you know, the more money I wanted. I had people in Brooklyn, Manhattan, the Bronx, Boston, in upstate. All I was basically doing was gettin' the drugs and receiving the money.

The "career" trajectories of the women in the preceding accounts reflect the influences of structure and context in shaping their choices and options. With limited access to legal work, and in segregated neighborhoods with high concentrations of joblessness, alienated views of legal work and diminished expectations for conventional employment became normative. For some of the women, the criminal involvements of family and friends were more likely to integrate them into the criminal world than into referral networks for legal employment. For others, youthful criminal acts marginalized them, at the outset, from interest in or access to job contacts that would initiate and sustain legitimate occupational careers.

But for those women who had some experience in the secondary labor market, commitment to criminal careers ended their involvement in the legal workaday world. Denise, who earlier described her job experiences, told us about her break with marginal labor:

Well, I still went from job to job pulling new scams. Worked for some lawyers and ran a prostitution thing out of their office. But after a while, it didn't work. So, like I discovered a new scam. I quit working for the lawyers and with my two babies of my own and I got on welfare. Once I had that system figured out, I took the bus over to another town, and, uh, I got on welfare out there. I used a wig and glasses, somebody else's baby, and I had a birth certificate printed up with my name, and I go on welfare out there too. I tried this from town to town. I was collecting numerous checks. It was good money.

But there was more money to be made. About when I was 20, I started to sell drugs with my father and uncle. I made about $1500 a day! Well, see, $500 goes back into the business, and clothes, hotels, men, friends. I dealt heroin for about 2 years. Then I went into business for myself. I wanted the money to go for myself. I sold heroin and coke. I also got back into prostitution. I had a house that became my father's rival. Because of the house, the girls only had to give me like $200. They made between $600 or $700 a night. You know what I'm sayin'. I just wanted $200 and that was it, 'cause I know how the hustle goes. I was clearing $4500 to $5500 a week.

I was still running my business, my old business, but it wasn't lucrative enough; cause people . . . it was like crack then. So I got turned on to it. I had to look at it like, well, how can I like turn this into money, not only get high, but to maintain my style. I met this man, this old man, and he taught me how to cook up coke, how to bottle it, and how to sell it. For the first month, I only made like, just about $1000. Just enough to re-up and to buy me an outfit. And that wasn't good enough for me. Before I knew it, I was sellin'. I was makin' $6500 per week, if not better. Then I got workers.

I had workers in the street, and at night I had another house that they'd work out of, uh, as long as I paid the girls' rent, which is only $250. Nobody sold out of my house. I couldn't have police comin' here. I had 10 people that worked for me. I had 5, let me get it right, I had 4 runners. Four muscles, very strong and very capable people. And 2 people that sat in the house with me. The muscle was generally the men. The others were girls I went to school with, girls I trusted, girls I did shit with.

For other women, especially those in the late-onset group, drug use exerted a strong influence on their ultimate commitment to the illegal economy over employment in the secondary labor market. Even at the outset, commitment to licit work was weak. But with the onset of cocaine smoking, such investments diminished and quickly disappeared. Barbara's involvement in legitimate work ended with her abuse of crack:

I worked for the Board of Education as a teacher's aide from like '84 to '86. When I was working I didn't need to be involved in crime at that time because I had my own income. But I was smoking crack. I was fired from the Board of Ed. because of my lateness and absenteeism. I went back on welfare.

I got so involved in getting high that I was kind of glad that I didn't have to get up in the morning anymore. I didn't care about that job or those people on that job, or even the kids like I was supposed to. I didn't care about a lot of things, and I preferred layin' home and waitin' for a check to come even as it was much less than what I was gettin' from the Board of Ed. It was like $400 compared to $150. That's when I started gettin' into crime.

Usually people start boostin' when they in they 14s or 15s, but after the Board of Ed., that's how I got money. I was pretty damn good at it. I also use to go get money for my WIC checks. I could sell them instead of usin' them. I use to steal welfare checks and cash them in. I rip off houses, even my mother's house. I sold everything in my house. I snatch pocketbooks and jewelry. Occasionally, I would get involved in selling my hide. Like if somebody was sellin' it, I would get involved with them for that night. But sometimes I used to stand on the corner and pick people up.

I never went back to working legal once things ended with the Board of Ed. I was only interested in how to make a living through hustles and scams. And, I was only interested in getting the money for the crack.

As we have heard, entry into cocaine smoking intensified the illicit activities in which they already were active. Evelyn recalls the following:

What happen was I didn't have any money, I didn't have any way of getting a job, I was already addicted into crack. Like I said, my parents threw me out of the house, there was no way of getting any money from them or anything like that; I had bumped into people who were selling, and I got connected with them Two Spots selling drugs with their bosses. I said can I help you out, be your lookout or whatever, and from there I started working and I met the bosses and I started working like that.

I would look out for them, and I say listen I will look out for your back if you give me so and so. They didn't want you smoking when you were selling, they wanted you to get rid of their stuff, and then you could smoke after you finished selling their stuff; if not you would get physically hurt.

Although the women's stories show that illicit behaviors were continuous over time, their intensification suggests transitions to new phases of deviant careers. These phases were structured by social opportunities and exogenous factors such as developments within drug markets. The development of the cocaine economy created opportunities for drug selling that did not exist in the smaller, more stable heroin markets. The changing economic structure of inner-city neighborhoods also created the possibility of changes in gender roles that in the past determined options for status and income within street drug networks.

At one time, women were excluded from selling by rigid gender roles and male hegemony in deviant street networks. The expanding cocaine economy and the increasing presence of women in the public domain may have neutralized the social processes that in the past consigned them to secondary roles in street networks. As a result, the women were able to form new organizations for drug selling or pursue independent careers in drug selling.

For Gayle, making money through drug selling was her career ambition:

I sold all kinds of drugs. I knew from the start that I wanted to be big in this. From weed I went to selling heroin and to coke. I started dealing weed at 15. I used to steal weed from my father and deal it. Somebody approached me to deal crank (speed). I was making $200 a week. This guy provided the speed. I sold in this parking lot where kids hung out. I made $800 to $900 a week from speed.

Then I sold heroin. I already had the knowledge of dealing. I went straight to somebody who sold heroin. The idea was strictly to make money. I knew a guy who sold heroin. At first I sold it myself. Then I would cut ounces and bag it and let my female friends sell it for me off the street. I was making $2500 a week. I dealt heroin for years and I started dealing coke. At this point I really learned how to make lots of money selling drugs.

I just got out of prison, and I asked my sister how much it would cost to start a business. She said $500. I got a grand from my husband. I bought two ounces of cooked-up crack. Opened this place at one of my sister's friends' house. I already mastered a plan for it. I didn't have to pay her cash for the apartment. She was strung out on crack, so I just paid the girl crack. I started making good money. I wasn't using crack at the time. I did try it about a year later.

There was about eight of us—seven women. I always had a dream to have an all-women crew. Whether people realize it or not, women sell drugs more easily than men. More people approach you because you are a woman. But women don't like to be known selling drugs, so sometimes they have a male front. There are a lot of women drug dealers. They have males to front off for them, to keep the attention off of them. You have to have some protection over yourself. A man who they believe is the boss.

Viewing women's involvement in drug markets in economic and career terms suggests an active role in decision making. Earlier deterministic conceptions of women and drugs described a passive drift into the secondary roles of hustling and prostitution in a street world dominated by men. However, the accounts provided by the women in this book indicate that within contemporary drug markets, women made decisions to participate based on a logical evaluation of career options. Here, the women considered both economic (wages) and nonpecuniary (status) returns from work in the secondary labor market. Furthermore, they realistically assessed their chances of obtaining economic and social support from domestic arrangements. Recognizing their constrained options, these women opted for illicit work that to them seemed to represent a rational choice.

Stephanie's account reflects this weighing of options:

> Well I've been working off and on in different cashiers and stuff like since I'm 15 years old. I always knew that a woman couldn't depend on a man to take care of her. I grew up on Public Assistance. I saw how it affected my mom when we on PA. People always coming to check up on your home. And then I remember going all the way down somewhere, someplace she had to go to be interviewed for something, but I remember her sitting in front of these people and she began to cry. And, and I just couldn't understand why they were putting her through all this. And I know it was about money. It was about money for her children. And that hurt me, I never liked going through that. I hated having to go to the "face-to-face." I hated even the phrase.
>
> So I knew I would have to get a career or something. But work was just menial jobs to me, and they really didn't matter. I never liked, really liked clerical work and the sittin' down jobs. I left after about 2 years and did hair. But that was not getting me anything.
>
> Shoplifting was a real big, a big high for me. Even after a day of work and making good tips, I still shoplifted. Occasionally I forged a few checks. But shoplifting basically was like, that was just, that became in the blood after a while. I really got high off of getting over in stores and things; and many times I had plenty money in my pocket, and I would still go and steal things. People noticed how fine I was looking. People also noticed my talent for taking stuff. I was getting a reputation, respect, on the street.
>
> But then I saw that dealing drugs was a way to make real money. I wasn't goin' to be on PA. I started freelancing. I purchased coke from a guy that I used to cop for myself. He had a lot of influential people used to come and cop drugs from him. So I began to bring people to him. So at first I was like a steerer. But since I still had a job, in the hair business there's a lot of drugs flowing. So I used to just buy in large quantities and sell to people at work. I sold to people I knew, who I knew were into drugs. They would get it from me right then and there. And this went on during the course of the day. When I got off from work, I usually went to a friend's house that I know got high. I sat and got high with them, and I usually sold to whoever was in their home.

For Stephanie and many of the other women, criminal career choices provided them with higher incomes than were reachable

by their peers in conventional careers. Furthermore, their involvement and success in these career trajectories placed them in contexts offering status (Hanson et al., 1985; Williams, 1989; Padilla,
1992), excitement (Adler, 1985; Anderson, 1990), and commodities
otherwise unavailable to them.

Drug selling also augmented the routine involvement of these
women in a variety of hustles such as fraud, larceny, and theft
(Johnson et al., 1985; Hunt, 1990; Murphy et al., 1991). For other
women, drug selling was an extension of already developed illegal
careers and an opportunity for increasing their crime incomes.

Further, their involvement in drug distribution also provided
opportunities for prostitution. This was especially true for cocaine
and crack markets (Chin and Fagan, 1990; Hamid, 1990; Bourgois,
1989; Goldstein, Ouellet, and Fendrich 1992; French, 1993; Inciardi
et al., 1993). And this was certainly true for the women with whom
we spoke. Forty percent of them said they were involved in prostitution, and 72 percent of these women began their participation
only after having become addicted to crack.

But involvement in the sex markets that emerged from crack distribution and use was phenomenologically different from more
traditional forms of prostitution. Within the context of cocaine and
crack markets, the sex trade has been characterized by tremendous
and volatile disorganization (Ratner, 1993). Confrontations among
sellers over rampant price-cutting, "viccing" (robbing customers),
and more abusive sex practices have been far more common in
crack sex trade markets than in other contexts of prostitution
(Ouellet et al., 1993; Maher and Curtis, 1993).

These changes, in turn, have had a profound effect on inner-city
neighborhoods. The higher levels and new types of degradation,
victimization, and desperation that characterize these sex-for-crack
experiences have spilled into the streets of distressed neighborhoods. All residents, law abiding or not, have been affected. They
are forced to witness public displays of the humiliation, disgrace,
and debasement that crack-addicted prostitutes undergo. They have
been forced to suffer from an unprecedented increase in violent victimization, HIV infection, and venereal disease (Althaus, 1991, cited
in Bourgois and Dunlap, 1993:123) that have emerged out of the pro-
liferation of desperate sex trade activities. Their emergency rooms
are filled beyond capacity with the casualties of these forces.

The women described in this book were all too keenly aware, by observation or by their own experience, of the havoc brought about through the spread of crack and its ancillary markets. The portrayals that they provided were eerily uniform and consistent with the descriptions already found in the literature. Tina and Patricia, for instance, spoke to us about the price-cutting that characterized the sex-for-crack market:

> Normally you try to ask for fifteen dollars for a blow job. These girls do it for five or less. That's, that's, you know, self-degradation. You can't blame the men because of course if you can get a blow job for five instead of ten or fifteen, you're going to take it. It's like someone selling me a bag of dope for five dollars; of course I'm going to buy your dope instead of the dope for ten, you know. (Tina)
>
> Yeah, we got a girl we call "Two Dollar Mindy." She go out . . . Mindy will stay with a date 45 minutes and come back and she wanna get down on [share] crack. Two Dollar Mindy don't care about nobody, nuttin'—long as she got two dollars. On a good date she got four—she come back and she need a dollar. Why would you pick up a girl for ten when you can get one for two? (Patricia)

But price-cutting was only one of the problems that arose out of these markets. The expanded sex markets and the compulsive patterns of crack use also increased women's risks of victimization for money or sex; for at the same time, the disorganization characteristic of crack sex markets eroded the traditional structures of protection—pimps on the street and madams in the brothels. These "guardians" have been replaced by drug dealers or operators of crack houses (Goldstein et al., 1992), who, unlike traditional pimps and madams, have little "concern" for the immediate health and welfare of their workers. As a result, the crack-addicted prostitutes with whom we spoke recounted horrid tales of victimization. Yvette, who walked the streets alone, desperately seeking any opportunity to obtain crack, provided us with the following account:

> This crack makes people fearless at certain points and also gives you a "you don't give a fuck" attitude. So you know, they will hurt you, they really will. And you have no one lookin' out for you. One time, this happened around twelve at night. Around midnight, this guy I know, he only came with nine dollars, and asked if I could do him for nine dollars. But he doesn't wait for me to answer. I would have done him

for anything. So he says to me, since he doesn't wait for the answer: "Since you can't do it for nine dollars, I'm gonna take everything"; and he took my crack. He pushed me against the wall and I was fightin' him. So he punched me and cut my eye open. I got ten stitches. He had a cane and he hit me with the cane. He broke it over me. Then, he body-slammed me. Then he started hitting me with the cane until my eye was messed up. He took, uh, sixty dollars and four vials.

The women in our study were acutely cognizant of these dangers. For the 60 percent who reported never having been involved in prostitution and even for those who drifted in and out, the opportunities for producing income through drug selling reduced their overall involvement in sex markets (Sommers, Baskin, and Fagan, 1996). We found that, especially during periods of increased drug use, drug dealing activities obviated other nondrug crime activities as well as involvement in legal work and receipt of public transfers. For the majority of the women, then, dealing was the preferred source of income support, particularly in order to purchase drugs.

The increased involvement of women in drug markets as sellers, manufacturers, crew bosses, and so on is clearly a phenomenon of the crack market. During prior drug eras, women were excluded from any real participation, especially within heroin markets. Women heroin users were viewed typically as unstable, promiscuous, and unreliable (Rosenbaum, 1981; Colten and Marsh, 1984; Stephens, 1991; Erickson and Murray, 1989), thereby effectively cutting off their participation even in illegal economic activities and social circles. As a result, their daily life was characterized by constant hustling, scoring, and doing heroin (Rosenbaum, 1981) at the exclusion of contact with other street deviant groups. Thus, women heroin addicts were marginalized from opportunities to become involved in drug dealing or other criminal enterprises, except for prostitution.

For women heroin users of past drug eras, then, crimes that have come to be associated with gender, such as prostitution and, tangentially, forgery and fraudulent check cashing dominated during their drug use careers. Stagnation in these crime patterns was reinforced by gender roles within networks of street drug users and by the physiological effects of injected opiates. Men initiated women into heroin use (Stephens, 1991; Blom and van den Berg, 1989), sold heroin to them (Rosenbaum, 1981), and were their pimps. Men also effectively excluded women from drug dealing (Rosenbaum, 1981; Valentine, 1978; Miller, 1986; Hunt, 1990), limiting them to an occasional role as "holders" of drug supplies (Goldstein, 1979). Thus, working in the drug markets of the heroin era was a less attractive economic choice than prostitution, hustling, fraud, or theft.

The development of a cocaine economy created opportunities for women in drug selling that did not exist in the smaller, more stable heroin markets. The changing social and economic structures of inner-city neighborhoods also created the possibility of changes in the gender roles that in the past constrained women's options for status and income within street drug networks. At one time, women were excluded from selling by rigid gender roles and male hegemony in deviant street networks. The expanding cocaine economy neutralized these social processes that in the past consigned them to secondary roles in street networks. The combination of these factors enabled women either to circumvent gender roles in street drug networks and form new drug selling organizations or pursue independent careers in drug selling.

Selling helped many women avoid the types of street hustling, including prostitution, that characterized women's income strategies in earlier drug eras. In the past, the worlds of drug use, drug dealing, prostitution, theft, and other hustles composed the "life" of people within active street networks (French, 1993; Bourgois and Dunlap, 1993). Illegal businesses providing goods and services historically formed the heart of the economy of the "life." Whereas women were consigned secondary, gender-specific roles in these businesses in the past, the size and seemingly frantic activity of the current drug markets helped create new ways for women to participate in street networks. Their involvement in drug selling at high income levels defied the gendered norms and roles of the past, when drug dealing was an incidental income source often mediated by domestic partnerships. The expansion of drug markets in the cocaine economy has provided new ways for women to escape their limited role, status, and income of previous eras.

The women's declining income share from legal work suggests that their attachments to licit labor markets were easily broken as their involvement in cocaine selling intensified. Their low educational levels and short work histories made high incomes from legal work generally unattainable. Rather than being drawn from licit work to drug selling, women who chose to sell drugs had few skills that were attractive to putative employers in a service or skilled labor economy. Legal work was a weak option for income, and drug selling seemed to be an appropriate match for this surplus labor pool. Recent data on the declining economic position of even full-time workers further explain women's decisions to pursue illegal incomes that significantly exceed their expectations from legal work (*New York Times*, 1994). Drug incomes also were higher than those of other types of crime.

Nevertheless, the highly gendered social networks of earlier eras persist in the cocaine economy. Like heroin addiction, crack use seems to result in immersion in a social world where options become narrower and exploitation more likely (Rosenbaum, 1981). The narrowing options seem to reflect both the social contexts in which crack is used and the effects of the drug itself. Similar to heroin use in past eras, heavy crack use seems to close off social exits from drug use or hustling. One woman said that the intense pleasure from smoking crack, and the reinforcement when it was repeated, made it impossible "to make any space between [herself] and the world where [she] smoked it." Reinarman et al. (1989) described the isolation that accompanies obsessive crack use, the suspicions toward friends and family members, the withdrawal from social interactions, the rejection of activities that do not lead to refilling the pipe, and the cashing in of limited economic and social assets in pursuit of an elusive but mythically powerful high.

In the social context of crack use, it is not surprising that street crime, including prostitution, continued to be an important part of the "life" and an important income source for the women who used crack. For many of the women, initiation often led to deeper immersion in the social scenes and behaviors that limited their participation in both street and conventional social networks. Although some walked away from crack after experimentation or maintained limits on their use of crack, others immersed themselves in crack use and reconstructed their social and economic lives to accommodate their frequent crack use.

The points of immersion into crack markets as users and as sellers were important turning points in all spheres of life for the women in our study. Their *economic* lives, for instance, became increasingly intertwined with their *social* worlds. They became marginalized from legal work and disdainful of prostitution. They organized their lives around drugs and immersed themselves in activities with people with whom they shared economic and social behaviors. Their roles and identities, as well as their primary sources of status and income, became defined, exclusively, within these street networks. Their options for transition to legal work, marriage, or educational settings were limited. And their engulfment in street networks reinforced their pathway into the abyss.

Notes

1. It is important to reiterate the point here that these women still maintained some commitment, although tenuous, to some conventional activities. Their engulfment in the deviant world was not yet complete.

2. It is important to note here that we, like Wilson (1996:70), recognize the presence of prosocial conduct in ghetto neighborhoods. And, the fact that the women sought licit employment attests to their initial commitment to this "mainstream value." However, the overwhelming disorganization and distress that are prevalent in these areas allow "unflattering behaviors" to prevail so that "the transmission of these modes of behavior . . . is more easily facilitated" (Wilson, 1996:71) and attenuation of bonds to these values eroded.

3. It is worth noting that during the interview, whenever we reached the theme of work history, the women were much less animated and enthusiastic in their accounting. Almost any other topic brought much more eagerness and interest. The blandness of their attitudes toward work in many ways mimics the lack of interest society-at-large has for these jobs. If we imagine being at a party and asking the perennial question—so what do you do for a living?—when the answer is, I'm a supermarket cashier, the one asking the question turns the other way and finds someone else with whom to talk. Much the same can be said for our reaction if our offspring were to bring home a potential significant other whose "career" was in the secondary labor market.

Chapter Five

The What, Where, When, Why, and Who of Violent Events

Up to this point, we have focused on the women's pathways into violent offending and the effects that drugs, peers, family, and community had on their decisions to become involved. Once involved in violent offending, however, the women were faced with choices and decisions that had to be made about their participation in individual crime events.

Therefore, in this chapter, we turn our attention to the effects that situational or microlevel factors had on their experiences with committing violence. In other words, we explore with the women what factors influenced their decision to participate in a particular event (motivation); what, if any, elements of rationality or planning went into the commission of the crime; how they decided whether to include other people or weapons and, if so, which people and what types of weapons; whether drugs or alcohol were ingested either prior to or during the event; and how they decided where to commit the crime. We also explore such interactional aspects as victim-offender relationships and accomplice involvement. Through the accounts that the women provided, we hear how they describe and justify their involvement in two particular violent crimes, robbery and assault.[1]

Robbery

Motivations to Commit Robbery

Me and my friend, we'd hang out. No big activity. We'd hang out in the project. Just like everyone else, no different. I had one best friend. Whatever we did, we did together. We loved to have fun, to go on adventures. First, we'd get high, we do a little robbin'. Take things from people, sell it, buy our reefer. You know what I'm saying. Robbin' was part of the fun. We got off on it. . . . When crack came out, yeah, it was gunfire. You know, uh, dealing in the hallways, people getting high in the hallway, you know what it was like. But you just adjust to it. It's just in your environment and you learn to work with it. No big deal. Everyone's somehow in it. You're either selling it and using it, robbing or stealing to get it, or hanging with people who are. It's something you just go with. Robbin' became a part of workin' with it. It's everyday stuff. Not as exciting but still part of the hustlin', partyin', and getting what you need. (Denise)

Typically, robbery has been characterized as an instrumental offense (Feeney, 1986). It has been portrayed as "similar to other property crimes with respect to its principal motive" (Cook, 1990:93) of obtaining money or some other desired valuable (Cook, 1990; Feeney, 1986; Megargee, 1982). For these women, such a view would be too unidimensional and static. Upon initiation into robbery, the majority of the women we spoke to stated that they became involved for adventure, excitement, and social interaction. This was especially true for the women in the early-onset group. Denise's account was typical:

When I first started, it was for fun. I was 15. I wanted to be down with the group. We'd just take things. If I saw it, I took it: chains, jewelry, stuff like that. It wasn't if I needed it. It was just something fun that we would do.

Dawn, too, became involved in robberies as a "social" activity:

Yeah, we'd cut outta school and hang for a while. But then we'd get bored and look for something exciting to do. We'd go to the park and stick people up, see their faces, see how surprised they were. Sometimes we'd go into stores and stick them up. Then we'd take the stuff we got and go and party.

Thus, early participation in robbery was based primarily on non-pecuniary motivations. Thrills, excitement, and peer pressure have all been cited in the research literature as factors related to male initiation into robbery (Cook, 1990; Katz, 1991; Petersilia, Greenwood, and Lavin, 1977). However, down the criminal career path, economic motivations came to dominate.

This was certainly the case with the women we interviewed. Although initial participation in robbery by the women in the early-onset group was based on noneconomic motivations, their subsequent involvement was of an instrumental nature. They came to join the women in the later onset group in committing robbery for an instrumental reason—in order to obtain the resources necessary to buy drugs. This shift in motivation is expressed by Denise, who has already shared with us her statement concerning the expressive roots of her involvement:

> So, yeah, it started as fun. But then I got into drugs and I did it to get money to party and get high. So it then became both—fun and drug money. But then I got a habit and I did robberies in order to take care of my habit—for nothing else. It is money for drugs, drugs. I was shooting morphine-based dope. I would use like a bundle and a half of dime bags. So that's like $150, that was just on the heroin. I would do the speedball with it so I had to get cocaine, that was about $80. Then I would have to have my methadone because I would have to come down. That was, maybe, $20 to $25.

By the time we interviewed the women for our study, the majority of the most recent robbery events (89 percent) were motivated by the need for money. Of these events, 81 percent were being committed to support a drug habit. This was clearly the case for Dawn, a 32-year-old African-American from Central Harlem, who turned from an occasional involvement in robbery as an early-onset offender to heavy involvement owing to her desperate need for crack money.

> Yeah, all of it then became drug-related because other than that I didn't need that kind of money. The money go immediately to buy more drugs. And you always need to "work" to get more money.
> Robbing people was a joke. I thought everything was funny 'cause I was on drugs, you know. I didn't care. I needed money for crack.

Janelle, too, was driven to serious involvement in robbery by her addiction:

> I was at the hospital, I was sick. I was trying to get admitted, I was real sick. Because of my habit, I was all swolled up, my kidneys were messed up. I was in bad shape. I had got so low that I slept on a rooftop that night before. When I got to the hospital, I saw the gold chains around the girl's neck. I said, I can get them without hurting her.
>
> I knew she had money and she's telling me she don't have no fuckin' money. It is like this demon or something came over me 'cause I wanted a hit. And I just snatched her damn chain and pocketbook.

The role that substance abuse played in changing the character of these women's involvement in criminality cannot be underestimated. It is important to note that, for the majority of the women we interviewed (66 percent), the perpetration of robbery occurred in the course of and subsequent to a criminal career that included involvement in other offenses such as nonviolent theft or vice.[2] Thus, the women in our study who were involved in robbery were not crime specialists but had a history of engagement in nonviolent theft, fraud, forgery, prostitution, and drug dealing.

What of the remaining 19 percent of the women we spoke with for whom robbery was unrelated to drugs? For them, the desire for excitement, vengeance, and friendship formed the basis of their actions. As Darlene related,

> It wasn't like I had to do these things, even with my drug habit. I didn't have to commit no crimes because my son's father had the coke and I always could get the clothes, money, and drugs from him. I did robberies because my peers who I was hanging out with was into these things. And that's what I decided to do. I wanted to be with my friends.

And what did they do with the money? The majority used the money to purchase clothes, jewelry, or electronic equipment. Their purchases, by their own admissions, often exceeded their needs or abilities to use these items. One woman told us that she had five VCRs sitting in her mother's apartment and a "whole lot of jewels" lying around even though she didn't even like to wear jewelry. Instead, she reported having fun buying the stuff as part of the social life she shared with her accomplices.

Occasionally, the women with whom we spoke engaged in robbery out of vengeance. Jackie, for instance, did not think of herself as trying to rob at all. She was attempting to recover money she claimed was owed her. Her motivation was to get what she thought belonged to her.

> The lady owed me money 'cause I had gave her money for a bottle of methadone and she never gave me the methadone. She sold me some garbage. So when she got her check, I went there to get my $50 back. She called the cops. It wasn't really robbery.

In many ways, the choice of robbery as a means of meting out "justice," having fun, and obtaining expensive commodities, or as a way of obtaining money for drugs, fits in with the deviant character of these women's social lives in general. And it is precisely within this deviant subculture that robbery is seen as "a routine matter analogous to going shopping" (Katz, 1991:288).

Equally routine and indicative of their readiness to use violence, particularly in a robbery (70 percent of the events included weapons use), is the fact that 60 percent of the women interviewed carried weapons on a regular basis. And 60 percent ($N = 62$) of these women were involved in both robbery and assault. This should not be surprising. For the idea that crime in general and crimes of violence specifically are associated with other lifestyle patterns has been well documented (Gabor et al., 1987; Katz, 1991; Shaw, 1966; Thomas, 1974). Given the neighborhood context in which these women were socialized, it was not unusual to find that violence was a normative part of the overlapping social networks in which these women participated.

Planning and Decisions Concerning Targets

Perhaps as an outgrowth of the more generally deviant lifestyles led by these women, in which there is daily movement in and out of a network of illicit activities (e.g., drug buying and selling, vice, nonviolent theft), many reported taking a very casual approach to their robberies. Eighty-three (54 percent) of the robbery events involved no planning at all. The spontaneous, spur-of-the-moment nature of many of these robberies is depicted in the following account:

We didn't plan nothing, we just plan to go out to make money. It was something, it was exciting to see if you could get over.

I was in the laundry mat at the time the money was taken, but I did not take the money myself, because there were two girlfriends of mine that was there, they were doing crack. I left my jacket, but I did not pick up the $73 in quarters that the woman alleged that I have taken. But I did pull the knife. It just happened. I wasn't on crack. Crack was sold out of that laundry mat. I did pull the weapon on the woman but did not take the money. The women saw my friends take the money and came after them. I pulled the knife and we ran out.

The degree to which an offense is "planned" has been the focus of recent debate (Clarke and Cornish, 1985). Some researchers suggest that criminal decision making is highly rational, following a sequential course from the decision to offend to the selection of the target (Bennett and Wright, 1984; Brantingham and Brantingham, 1984; Walsh, 1980). Most current work, however, assumes that individuals seek to maximize utility, but within limits posed by the incompleteness and uncertainty of the information available to them (Clarke and Cornish, 1985; Cook, 1980).

Others view criminal decision making as primarily a product of opportunity (Cohen and Felson, 1979; Rengert and Wasilchick, 1985). In a study of residential burglary, Cromwell et al. (1991) concluded that most burglaries resulted from the exploitation of opportunity rather than from careful, rational planning. They suggested, however, that opportunism does not necessarily imply a lack of rationality. An offender may make a completely rational decision to take advantage of certain opportunities when they arise or to seek out opportunities in a systematic manner.

The women we interviewed demonstrated only limited rationality in the commission of robberies. In only 46 percent of the robbery events was any planning involved. And among these events, 66 percent of the planning involved thinking about where to commit the crime, whom to target, or both. Even so, these aspects of planning generally occurred only within a short time, usually a few minutes but sometimes a few hours, before the actual event. As Wanda reported,

We'd usually go to the park stickin' up people. I knew I was going to do it. If I took my gun out, I knew what I was going to do. Yeah, I would look for easy people. People who looked timid, who ain't gonna put up much of a fight.

April, too, spoke of how limited, even nonexistent, the planning was:

You know, we knew we was goin' up there to stick somebody up, but we wasn't gonna be like let's rob her, I know her, or stuff like that. We just did it, just, you know, whoever we saw.

Barbara summarizes this lack of forethought:

Well, once the gun was bought, you might say it was planned, but, you know, as far as who and where, no. That was kind of spontaneous. You just have to have an eye open for that type of thing.

Having an eye open, taking advantage of an opportunity, all of these descriptions are suggestive of a very limited rationality in terms of the planning of the robbery events. Perhaps more characteristic of the "nature" of their planning was when they fell into a pattern. As Darlene describes,

I would do a robbery maybe every 2 weeks or so. A couple of times it was street robberies, but most times it was men I'd set up. Lots of times I would go to their houses—I planned the robberies—they were always the same. A friend would tell me about a certain person and would give me the address and everything. They would tell me where the stash was, it could be money, jewelry, drugs, whatever. I'd go over there and meet this guy, introduce myself, and rob him. I would do this every couple of weeks. It got to be quite a good routine.

Consistent with their generally casual attitude toward planning was their choice of victim. Data from the present study show the robbery victims were most frequently strangers (72 percent). The impersonality of female robbery conforms with the existing literature on male robber-victim relationships (Feeney, 1986; Le Blanc and Frechette, 1989). Yet contrary to existing findings (Hindelang, 1976), robbery victims in the present study were as likely to be males as females. This held true except for events in which weapons were *not* used. In these cases, women were more likely to rob other women.

The typical way for the respondents to choose their victim was by what they called "intuition." They frequently reported waiting for a target who "looked right" or who looked "weak" and vulnerable. For example, Jocorn reported the following:

> I would look for a certain type of person and I would plan what I was gonna say and when I was gonna make my move. I was looking for, uh, alcoholics, people who were coming out of bars and drunk. They were an easy target. And they were always so many of them in the neighborhood.

Stephanie had a routine in which she waited for paydays and times of the month when people received transfer payments:

> Yeah, it was always the same times of the week or month; it depended if I was going to go after somebody with a job or a welfare person. I'd stick them up in the streets, you know, we know when they got paid, you know, welfare and social security checks, maintenance workers. I knew when they were carrying their money.

Looking out for a particular type of victim was typical for the women in our study. This was certainly the case for Alicia:

> You know I felt like if somebody looked soft or, you know, young people, they would have got stuck up. I always went after the same type of person with that soft look.

Sonya used to be on the lookout for potential victims:

> I'd have this thing where I would watch people in bars and follow them. One time, I followed this guy and grabbed his tie and I swung it down to the ground. And, uh, he hit his head and that's when I took the money and ran.

As already reported, the majority of these robberies were committed against strangers. It should be noted, however, that 19 percent of the robberies were committed against coparticipants in a particular drug scene. As L.G. told us,

> The people I hang out with were all drug addicts. I never really had friends. They were associates. We use to use each other to get drugs. Whatever I did was because I was into getting high. If I saw money or drugs I'd rip people off. Like one time I was getting off with some people in an alley, by a building I lived near, and this girl who was with us had some money. I just ripped her off. I was desperate. When I was desperate, I would rip anyone off—especially if they were already high.

TABLE 5.1   Motivational and Planning Characteristics of Robbery and Assault Events (percentages)

Characteristic	Robbery (N = 104, 154 events)	Assault (N = 88, 109 events)
Motivation		
Money	89	10
Excitement	5	7
Vengeance	6	10
Victim precipitation	–	72
Planning		
Yes	49	20
No	51	80
Victim-offender relationship		
Friend or acquaintance	9	61
Stranger	72	25
Drug relationship	19	14
Dealer	–	9
Customer	–	5
Drug user or partner	19	–

Note. Percentages are based on the number of robbery and assault events.

Generally, it could be said that the women in our study chose their victims in a very matter-of-fact way. For 54 percent of the robbery events, the women said they chose their victims because of convenience; for 28 percent, they said that the victims appeared to have money; and for 18 percent of the robberies, the women chose their victims because the risk appeared to be low (see Table 5.1).

Other Situational Aspects of Robbery

In addition to motivation and choice of target, location of the offense is an important situational component. The women reported that 60 percent of the robberies occurred in public areas including streets, parks, and subways. Thirty-two percent of the robberies occurred in quasi-public areas such as apartment building lobbies or hallways, typically in or near the women's own residence. And 8 percent of the robberies were in commercial locations.

To a large degree, the women's decisions about location could be understood in terms of Brantingham and Brantingham's (1984) concept of "awareness space." According to this idea, offenses are committed in areas that the person is familiar with by virtue of her daily movements when opportunities for crime become available within that space. Monica's account was typical of the women with whom we spoke:

> Yeah, I was always more comfortable doing it in the park. Yeah, there may have been people around, but I hung out a lot there and knew my ways in and out. People were there just hangin' and not paying enough attention. So I'd grab their stuff and be off. Or I would get them when they were going into the park, and I would just continue into the park while they were screamin'.

Or Janelle:

> Oh it was a big project. Lots of buildings. It was near the place I was staying. I'd wait in the hallways and find someone soft. Then I'd go down the stairs to another floor and be like nothing happened. Sometimes, I could get two or three of them in the same building one after another. I knew those buildings like I knew the back of my hand. I grew up with friends there when I was young.

In addition to choosing a location for the robbery, the women had to decide whether to use force or weapons. Research findings on robbery events indicate that these decisions represent a means of gaining control over the victim (Lejeune, 1977; Walsh, 1986). Cook (1976) has argued that robbers make choices according to (1) their own potency in generating a convincing threat and overcoming the victim's resistance and (2) their perception of the vulnerability and attractiveness of the victim. Although offenders can expect less resistance from vulnerable targets (e.g., relatively young or old victims), the "payoff" tends to be low. Offenders who select relatively well-defended targets that have a relatively high payoff may seek to increase their firepower by acquiring accomplices or deadly weapons (Walsh, 1986). Feeney's (1986) findings indicate that the use of weapons and force may be rationally calculated to gain swift control over an uncertain situation.

In our study, weapons tended to be used as a way of quickly defining the situation for the victim as a robbery as well as to manage or minimize victim resistance. Denise told us quite simply:

When you hold a gun, people don't argue with you. But when you hold up a knife, a man might try to fight you back. I didn't want to hurt anybody, but I wanted them to know I needed the money. I never had to use a weapon; they always gave it up.

Occasionally, however, violence was used to gain the "cooperation" of the victim. Respondents typically characterized this violence as precipitated by victim resistance, occurring in situations in which the victim failed to "give it up." As Janelle states: "We was robbin' her and she was like refusing. She resisted, so we beat this girl, we pistol whipped her. We had to do it so she'd give it up."

The need to use violence or at least its threat was prevalent. Seventy percent of the robberies involved the use of some kind of weapon: 27 percent involved guns; 38 percent knives or other sharp, cutting instruments; and 5 percent blunt instruments such as pipes or clubs. These incidents need not have been planned, for most of the women (66 percent) routinely carried a weapon. When used, the weapons were a means to intimidate the victims and gain control over the situation rather than to gratuitously produce harm or injury.

In further exploring the situational context of the robberies in which they participated, study women focused on the roles that they played vis-à-vis accomplices. Sixty-three percent of the robberies were committed with accomplices; 60 percent of these (38 percent of all robberies) involved female co-offenders, and 40 percent (25 percent of all robberies) involved male co-offenders. The remaining 37 percent of the robberies were committed alone. Women in the robbery sample reported that, from early on in their criminal careers, they acted out of self-determination and not in concert with or for boyfriends. Although the women sometimes were involved in criminal activities that involved men or activities that were controlled by men, they acted more often as equal partners.

These findings contradict much of the literature on female offending (cf. Campbell, 1984). Most of the available studies have focused on women as secondary actors in the crime event (Adler, 1985; Blom and van den Berg, 1989; Miller, 1986; Pettiway, 1987; Steffensmeier, 1983). By and large, it has been argued that women participate in criminal events in three basic ways. On the one hand, women act as lookouts while their men do the heavy and sometimes violent work

TABLE 5.2   Other Situational Characteristics of Robbery and Assault Events (percentages)

Characteristic	Robbery (N = 104, 154 events)	Assault (N = 88, 109 events)
Intoxication (drug/alcohol)	48	62
Offender role		
Alone	37	57
Others:	63	43
Male	25	13
Female	38	30
Location		
Public (street, park)	60	38
Quasi-public (hallways)	32	62
Commercial (stores)	8	–
Weapons		
Knife/cutting instrument	38	49
Gun	27	17
Blunt instrument	5	12
Strong-arm	30	15
Other	–	7

Note. Percentages are based on the number of robbery and assault events.

associated with criminal enterprise. A second scenario has women playing a passive role simply as holders or users of illegally obtained property or drugs. Finally, most of the available research has constructed a scenario in which women are engaged only as brow wipers who stand by their men to offer support services. These support services have been identified as ranging from fraudulent check cashing, prostitution, and other gendered types of criminal involvement to providing sex, food, and family for the criminally active male members of domestic and boyfriend networks (Adler, 1985; Blom and van den Berg, 1989; Miller, 1986; Steffensmeier, 1983). Accounts provided by the women in our study clearly contradict the established wisdom concerning women's roles in the perpetration of robbery offenses (see Table 5.2).

Assault

Motivations

Outside of research on "battered women who kill" (Browne, 1987) or on women who physically abuse their children (Garbarino,

1989), little is known about the situational dynamics of women's participation in assaultive behavior, especially against strangers. In general, research on the interactional processes leading to criminal violence is suggestive of a three-stage model for assaults. First, there is a verbal conflict in which identities are assailed and attempts to influence an antagonist fail. The second stage consists of threats and evasive action. Third, there is the physical attack in which retaliation appears to play a key motivational role (Campbell, 1984; Felson and Steadman, 1983; Luckenbill, 1980).

The accounts of Rhonda, Janelle, and Jackie are typical and reveal this process. As Rhonda states:

> I can recall, okay, I was walking home with my friend. There was this big fat girl who was arguing with another friend. I put my two cents in it. . . . Well, the next day I'm sitting in the laundry room—inside the projects—folding my clothes. So she came up to me and I look up and she's taking off her earrings. So I say what's up? So she says, yeah from last night. So I wheel my son over to my girlfriend on the next bench and the Clorox is right there. Right, so, I stand up and open the Clorox and I throw it in her face and she takes a sheet I had and she pull it up and I take the Clorox and I keep throwing it at her. It's all over her eyes, and she's still coming. She grabs the shopping cart, right, and I see a big stick. I pull the cart from her, and I constantly beat her with the stick and can't nobody stop me when I get at it, except the police. The police was called.

Janelle explains:

> My girlfriend wanted to go downstairs to make a phone call. So I said I can play my numbers too. The phone is right where I play my numbers. I go in the back and I ask the lady for a pen to write my numbers down. I write my numbers down but she didn't have change. So I go with the pen in my hand, I got some change. So there's this man arguing with somebody I knew. So I say, what's this noise all about? Then this man turn around and I can't remember the exact words that he said but he pushed, he did something to me physically. So I said if you ever put your hands on me again, I'll kill you. So I keep telling the man in the store this and that. So he leaves out the store and I'm on the way out of the store, right, and he comes back in and he says, bitch, I'll kill you, you know. So he goes in his back pocket, right, and I see he produced a lighter. So I said, you threatening me with a lighter, and I have the pen in my hand. I said, are you stupid? I said a few more words to him. All I know, all I can

recall, I am sticking him with the pen. He had an undershirt on and I sticked him with the pen and turned around and walked. Then I turned back and I sees this hole in his heart.

Jackie provided us with this account:

My sister called me over to watch the kids for a couple of hours. We were outside the project and people were hanging around on the bench. A friend of my sister's brought a dog along off the leash which scared the kids. I asked her to take the dog in or put it on a leash. She said, "I don't have to take the dog in, the kids been playin' with the dog." I said, "My nieces don't play with animals because they scared of them." We began arguing back and forth. "You nigger." "You fuckin' Puerto Rican." I sat down 'cause the baby was crying. She kept mouthing. She got up and charged me and I threw the baby on the floor. Then me and her was fighting. We was fighting for a long time. She had a razor and I went to grab it and she cut me. I got my key chain off my belt and cut her in her face and cut her again on her arm.

In dispute-related violence, the distinction between offender and victim is not necessarily clear. In some instances it is more accurate to describe the offender and victim as two antagonists and examine the routine activities that are likely to bring them together. If one or both have a proclivity to use violence, one expects that violent incidents are more likely (Felson, 1993). Take this account by Jocorn, for instance:

You know, there was one time this guy he, uh, was a glue sniffer. I was at my mother's house. I remember my little brother telling me, "Look Mommy's dancin' in the corner with some guy." I look out the window and this guy's ripping off my mom. I went down. By the time I went downstairs, he was gone. My mom managed to take a glass bottle and hit him over the head. But I asked her to describe him and he sounded familiar. I have a habit of not calling anybody for my fights, so I went straight over to his place. I did it on my own. I went with a gut feeling. I went up to his house, and I knew who it was. He was hiding in the closet sniffing glue. And I beat him down. And I had on boots and a chain, a leather chain.

In the previously cited events, as well as in most cases, the victim's actions were aggressive. This indicates that the victim in some way contributed to the outcome. However, the actions of the victims as reported both in the police reports and by the offenders themselves were not as aggressive as those of the respondents. Victims seem to physically attack less, and they more often engage in evasive actions.

Furthermore, although third parties were frequently present during an assault, the role that they played was principally as antagonist. Forty-three percent of the assault events occurred in the presence of others, but only in a few cases did third parties engage in the physical attack. More often, they participated in the verbal conflict. The presence of third parties appears to increase the perception that violence is legitimate, to increase face-saving concerns, and to increase the probability of retaliation.

Many women perceived their aggression as a form of retaliation for a previous wrongdoing against them. By retaliating, the women "saved face"—were able to nullify the image of being weak and ineffectual. This was certainly the case for Barbara:

> She stole my beeper a year ago. She came back to the block and started talking shit about my girlfriend's brother and my girlfriend. I went to the store to buy a beer and I was smoking a blunt. On the way back from the store I ran into her. So I asked her why she was running my name on the block. So I swung on her and she blocked it. She was a big girl, 5 foot 9, 300 pounds. I grabbed her by the coat and I punched her and she went down and I put a beating on her. I think I broke her nose, I messed her up real good. No way she was going to think I was soft. I knew when she stole my beeper that it was just goin' to be time before I set things right.

A common theme in many of the preceding accounts is that the use of violence is seen as a legitimate method to avenge being "dissed." It is an attempt to regulate other people's knowledge and opinions about oneself and one's friends. Anderson (1994:92) has discussed this phenomenon as part of the conflicts typical of young women in inner-city settings.

A major cause of conflicts among girls is "he say, she say." This practice begins in the early school years and continues through high school. It occurs when people, particularly girls, talk about others, thus putting their "business in the streets." Usually one girl says something negative about another in a group, most often behind the person's back. The remark then gets back to the person talked about. She may retaliate, or her friends may feel required to "take up for" her.

Thus, the quest for respect and honor leads many women to opt for a tough aggressive approach, enacting their own version of "manhood." As Anderson (1994:92) stated, "one of the most effective ways of gaining respect is to manifest 'nerve'." Nerve is shown when one takes another person's possessions, throws a first punch, or pulls a trigger.

Planning and Decisions

In many instances, particular aggressive actions (physical attacks, threats, identity attacks) on the part of the victim are associated with the same types of aggressive actions by the offender. These retaliatory actions are characteristically unplanned and evolve out of some personalized relationship with the victim. From the women's accounts, it was evident that the assaults were often impulsive and unorganized. Frequently, the women in our study reported that the event occurred during a state of intoxication. Often, they involved the use of dangerous weapons. Here, Darlene describes one such encounter:

> At the party he had gotten all drug up and everything. We went back to the bar, and I had no intention of him coming back to my apartment. To make a long story short, he took my keys out of my bag. Somebody told me he had taken the keys out of my bag and I wasn't paying attention, and then it dawned on me. I ran to the house. The guy had taken something from me before and that was another reason why I wanted to get rid of him. Now mind you this guy didn't live with me. He would come over on the weekends or whatever. Anyway when I got into the apartment these two very expensive pieces of jewelry was missing. I knew that they were there, because before I had left I had threw some pieces on the bed and they were not there. So, I was like get up and get out, I want you to leave. And he swore that he didn't take it. Anyway, he wouldn't leave, and I said if you don't leave I am going to call the cops. I reached for the phone he snatched the phone and pulled it out of the wall. We started to argue and kind of wrestled around. I said I want you out of my house, my stuff is missing. He said you better get out of my face before I smack you and this and that. I was standing here and he

kind of pulled me, this guy is 6 foot 3, 220. I am 5 foot 8 inches, 130 pounds, that ain't nobody to be messing with, anyway he went to put his hand up and I saw it coming. I saw a knife, something just said protect yourself and I grabbed it and I cut him. I stabbed him in his hand, but I was going to go for the arm or anyplace. It just happened.

Although the majority of assaults were unplanned (80 percent), the remainder did involve an element of forethought. These typically involved vengeance, related to either money or false accusations. Sonya's account, following, summarizes the rational intent of these incidents:

After I got out of jail, I still could not get over the fact that that woman had stood up in front of the police and gave positive ID of myself and my other neighbor. We were in the pen, they go and get her and said are these the two women that assaulted and robbed you in the hallway? Yes, these are the two women that assaulted me and robbed me. So when I got out of jail, I made bail, got out of jail, I go home, I slept, then I hear my neighbor, the women who IDed me, leaves to go out of the door, so I said let me explain something to you Miss, if you think I'm going to allow you to walk past my door, and its going to be all right when you falsely accused me of a crime I did not do, now what is it you said I did, assaulted and robbed you and that is exactly what's going to happen to you, and that's not a threat, that's a promise, I went back into my house and I closed my door.

I waited until she felt that was a false threat. I waited. Then she was talking about this and that one night, so I waited until 4 o'clock one morning, and I put on the coffeepot with the hot water, boiled the water, and I waited until she came out of her apartment and passed my door. I opened the door and she just froze because she didn't know what to expect; she didn't think mentally whether to go back to her apartment, so I took the 360 degree hot water, that was still bubbling, and just threw it right in her face. I didn't wait for a reaction, I just closed the door and got back in my bed.

Sonya's use of violence, like that of the other women in the study, was shaped by her surrounding environment and past experiences. Her proclivity toward aggression evolved in a defined subcultural space, in a street culture that set the rules for proper comportment and a proper way to respond if challenged.

Drugs and Assault

The tendency toward the routine use of violence became especially prominent with the expansion of crack markets. In the absence of any legitimate authority, violence was used to settle disputes and enforce discipline and boundaries. This relationship between drugs and violence has been observed in literally hundreds of empirical studies. People who use and sell drugs are more likely to engage in violence than non-drug-involved individuals. Accordingly, although women generally have low base rates of violence (Sommers and Baskin, 1992), their entry into drug use or selling increases the risks of violence.

As Goldstein (1985) has suggested, there are three ways that drugs and violence are related to each other: (1) The pharmacological effect of the drug on the user induces violent behavior; (2) the high cost of drug use impels users to commit compulsive violent crime to support continued drug use; and (3) violence as a common feature of the drug distribution system, which Goldstein calls *systemic violence,* serves a variety of purposes. Violence in this context is used to protect or expand drug distribution market share or to retaliate against market participants who violate the rules that govern transactions. As the following accounts indicate, the system of drug use and distribution creates a structure of situations conducive to retaliatory violence.

Sonya speaks of her use of violence to protect her drug dealing turf:

> I was involved in a lot of violence, a lot of physical violence. Sometimes I used weapons, a gun, a knife, with me it didn't matter, anything in my hand was a weapon. Somebody would get in my territory, I'd shoot at them and tell them to get off the corner, you know, that's how it was generally done. It became too much for me to handle alone, so I incorporated my boyfriend into my crew. Sometimes we had weapons. Usually women don't like to be known selling drugs so sometimes they have a male front. There are a lot of women drug dealers. They have males to front off for them, to keep the attention off of them. You have to have some type of protection over yourself. A man who they believe is the boss.

Stephanie describes the necessity for violence as self-defense:

I was selling up and down the block and these two guys went to rip me off. Right, they both approached me, and they kept askin' me what I had. I told them what I had. They kept sayin' let me see, let me see, like they were gonna take whatever I showed them, and I wouldn't. So I was grabbed from behind, and the guy that was standing in front of me, he grabbed my collar. And, I was already high and paranoid. And I slashed him. I slashed him with a razor. When I slashed him, his blood shot out. The other guy released me. There was blood everywhere. They let me go. Because of the sight of blood. And then most people didn't expect that type of thing from a person like me. That's why they tried.

Evelyn's use of violence was for the purpose of social control:

Well, there was this one girl. I had . . . it was coincidence, I happened to meet up with her here. I had taught her, ya know, cause she was selling drugs and the guys used to take advantage of her and I didn't like that. I despised that. So I took her home with me and I told her, "Look, this is what you're gonna do." And I was teaching her well. One day she went out and it was something she wasn't doing. She wasn't getting high. She came to me and she was $40 short of my money. And I asked her, "Where is my money?" She said, "Ma, look. I was hangin' out and they stole my money." And I got angry with her because of the fact that they played her out for her money. It wasn't that fact that she was short the $40, because I always give her more than that to take home. It was that fact that she let another crackhead come and play her out, when she should know their game. That's exactly why I bust her ass. Because I wanted her to learn.

Fights with buyers and sellers over bad drugs, and robberies of buyers and dealers, were the most prevalent forms of systemic violence. At times, violent interactions were an outgrowth of neighborhood resistance to drug dealing. Barbara describes one incident with a neighbor:

I was selling drugs in Manhattan, out of an apartment building. I was going downstairs when this guy says what are you doing here? He starts hassling me and pushes me. He says, "We don't wants drugs in this building." I never saw him before. He seemed high. I saw he had a knife in his hand. I had a .25 caliber. I was shot at twice while selling and I was robbed once. They were users. I always carry a .25. I shot him in the shoulder.

Overall, 26 percent of the women who sold drugs ($N = 115$, 68 percent of entire sample) were involved in systemic violence. Victimization, however, was a more likely violent experience than was commission of a violent act. Over half (57 percent) of the women who sold drugs, and over 1 in 3 women overall (38 percent), were victims of crime in the course of drug transactions. Rose describes an incident in Harlem:

Yeah, I was working and selling all day, see I was, like I said, when I first started freebasing I wasn't in it all heavy, it was just like, maybe after I worked I would buy like $50 worth and go home and smoke it and after that just go to bed. I use to make a lot of money when I use to sell dust. Like, maybe, thirteen or fourteen hundred dollars a day. People that observed and that be out there scheming on things, like that knew. And one night I was on my way home and I was living with my sister, I was walking through a building, I was going to this crack spot, pick me up some and go home. And um, these guys stopped me, it was three of them. They had the hats on with the eyes, I didn't really know what at the time was going to happen. They asked me if they could have a light, and I said no. And the other one grabbed me and said you do so and pulled out a gun on me. And I said I don't got nothing and I start to fight, and the guy hit me on the mouth with the end of it. And blood started gushing and I lost my teeth. It was hanging over, it was so big. And then I started getting frighten and they made me take off my clothes right in the middle of it, you know. And um, went all through my pockets, and cuz I had money all over, my shoes, my socks, my pants pocket, and shirt, and I had a leather bomber I had bought. And I had cut the pocket and puts my money all in my coat. And I had it with the pockets, it just doesn't feel like it was cut all around. You just put your hands in the pocket. The guys were going to take my clothes, and I said please don't take my clothes, you got the money so just go, you know. So I guess they felt sorry enough and left the clothes, and they ran and I put back on my clothes back on and I still had money in my coat, you know.

Interpersonal violence also occurred within the system of drug use. Alicia talks about one incident:

At age 17 I caught a case, attempted murder. It was dealing with drugs. We were hanging out and this guy got high over some angel dust. He flipped on me and we got into a fight. But he was tripping, and he and he was really trying to hurt me and I wind up stabbing him. It happened at his house. One minute everything was okay. The next minute, everything was all going crazy. He attacked me with a knife, and I grabbed the knife and I wound up hitting it away from him and I stabbed him and he died.

It is clear from the accounts provided by the women in our study that interactions between victim and offender and sometimes even the interaction (verbal) of a third party played a fundamental role in assault incidents. These women are not roaming willy-nilly through the streets engaging in "unprovoked" violence. They are frequently thrust in violence-prone situations in which the victim enters as an active participant, shares the actor's role, and becomes functionally responsible for it. Thus, in addition to Wolfgang's examples of victim-precipitation, cases in which "the victim was the first to show and use a deadly weapon" or "to strike a blow in an altercation" (1958:252), the present data suggest that the victim is functionally responsible for a great many more types of motivating behavior. The offender's conduct may be a result of open and direct provocation; it may be the outcome of an opportunity produced by the existence of the victim; or it may emerge in relation to the demands of the victim.

The women's accounts also suggest that criminal and deviant lifestyles directly increase victimization because of the nature of the offending behavior itself. As Jensen and Brownfield (1986) have argued, offense activity can be considered a characteristic of lifestyles or a type of routine activity that increases risk of victimization because of the vulnerability or culpability of people involved in those activities. Building on this idea, Sampson and Lauritsen (1990) examined the independent effect of violent offending behavior and deviant lifestyles on the risk of personal victimization. Their analyses showed that offense activity—whether violence or minor deviance—was directly related to the risk of assault, even when neighborhood levels of violence were controlled for. The common message throughout our data is that violent offending and violent victimization are intimately connected and that deviant lifestyles increase the likelihood of robbery and assault victimization.

The Context of Violence

Overall, the accounts provided by the women suggest that there are clear underlying differences in the perpetration of violent crimes. The women describe their involvement in robbery as more frequently planned, more impersonal, and more instrumental than their involvement in assault. However, these differences seemed to be more a matter of degree rather than categorical distinction. This became increasingly apparent as the interactional aspects of these perpetrations were explored.

Many of the decisions associated with robbery demonstrated a limited rationality (Walsh, 1980). Although the women involved in robbery did not calculate in the Bentham style, weighing and planning all angles, they did consider particular elements of the situation and disregard others, giving more attention to immediate critical factors. Assault, although typically characterized as an expressive criminal offense, was not without logic or reason. Each woman's actions were a function of the victim's behavior and the implications of that behavior for defending one's well-being or public self-concept. Thus, if we consider nonpecuniary goals (e.g., retaliation), then assault played a much more meaningful role in these women's lives than might have been anticipated.

From these women's accounts, it seems that violent female offenders are not a homogeneous group. In addition to differences in the underlying motivation or meaning of violence, there appear to be different behavioral patterns within the group of women with whom we spoke. Women who were involved in robbery, particularly robbery and assault, were disproportionately involved in other criminal activities, particularly drug sales, and were more deeply entrenched in addictive drug use.

Perhaps of greatest significance was the sense that whereas immediate situational factors differentiated robbery and assault incidents, there was tremendous overlap in the way in which all the study women conducted their lives. To varying degrees, the study women maintained membership in a variety of social worlds, including the worlds of family, work, drug use, and crime. Members of a social world have a common perspective on "reality" and share particular experiences and interests (Biernacki, 1986). Although the women were involved in various social worlds, the primary experiences and perspectives on "reality" shared by them rotated around a number of interrelated occurrences: obtaining money, often illegally; purchasing drugs; and using drugs.

For the majority of women, the problem of maintaining an addiction took precedence over other interests and participation in other social worlds. The women frequently defined themselves in relationship to their drug problems. They were "junkies," "crackheads," or "cokebitches." Few women, however, saw themselves as criminals. Their unscrupulous behaviors were justified by their "drug compulsion."

The increased salience or primacy of the deviant role for the individual has been described as "role engulfment." Schur pointed out that one major consequence of the processes through which deviant identity is ascribed is the tendency "of the deviator to become 'caught up in' a deviant role . . . that his behavior is increasingly organized 'around' the role . . . and that cultural expectations attached to the role come to have precedence in the organization of his general way of life" (Schur, 1971:69).

Adler (1985) utilized a similar concept in her description of the process of becoming a drug dealer. According to Adler, the process involves a progressive shift in identity as individuals become increasingly involved in the social networks of dealers. Joining the social networks requires a commitment to the drug world's norms, values, and lifestyle, and limits the degree of involvement with nondeviant groups.

As the circumstances of the women's lives changed, it became less and less likely that they actively considered alternatives to committing crimes. Decisions concerning the execution of violent crimes became routine or "patterned," relying largely on the women's ability to recognize and seize situational opportunities. The women's accounts tend to support Clarke and Cornish's (1985) rational choice framework which emphasizes the need to develop different decision models for involvement processes (beginning, continuing, and desistance) and the criminal event.

The women's accounts also are consistent with previous research findings that suggest that certain lifestyles and routine activities are associated with increased risks for offending and victimization (Cohen, Kluegel, and Land, 1981; Garofalo, 1987; Lauritsen, Sampson, and Laub, 1991). Further, they indicate that lifestyle factors (e.g., peer association, serious drug use) are associated with participation in robbery. Thus, the women's lifestyles and routine activities increased their probability of exposure to situations that were associated with more serious disputes leading to assaultive behavior.

As we have argued, these women are members of distinct communities that mediate between them and the larger economic and political organization. It is within local communities that the women interacted and made decisions regarding school, work, and family. And it is within these local communities that they devised ways of coping with the demands imposed by the larger structures. Community levels of family dysfunction, economic and social dislocation, as well as the presence of illegitimate opportunity structures provided the landscape for the lifestyles and routine activities that were related to the women's participation in violent street crime.

Notes

1. Of the 170 female offenders interviewed, 104 (61 percent) reported involvement in 154 robberies, and 88 (58 percent) reported involvement in 109 assaults. The range in the frequency of assaults was from 1 to 16, the median number was 3. Women varied greatly in the number of robberies they committed. Thirty-two percent ($N = 33$) said they committed only one robbery. However, 26 percent ($N = 27$) of the women reported frequent (> 10) involvement in robbery.

2. For example, of the women involved in robbery and addicted to drugs ($N = 102$), 40 percent ($N = 41$) were involved in burglary, 75 percent ($N = 77$) in drug sales, 55 percent ($N = 56$) in forgery, and 50 percent ($N = 61$) in prostitution prior to the addiction phase of their criminal offending.

Chapter Six

Getting Out of Crime and Violence

As we have seen in previous chapters, the trajectories of crime and drug behaviors for the women in our study reflected a shift in their social and economic relations. Their *economic* lives placed them increasingly in *social* worlds where they were distanced from legal work. Their everyday economic lives centered around the acquisition and consumption of drugs. They became immersed in street networks where their social interactions were increasingly limited to people involved in these economic and social behaviors. Their social roles and identities, as well as their primary sources of status and income, were increasingly defined within these street networks. In short, these women were locked into a deviant social world, having little stake in conventional life or conventional identity.

However, even the most persistent and lengthy criminal careers have a "natural" course, tapering off and eventually ceasing as the person ages, possibly "burning out" physically and easing out of "the life." In this chapter, we offer a glimpse into the lives of 30 of the study women who successfully exited the social world of violence, crime, and drugs.[1] We discuss a range of factors that affected their decisions to move out of deviance and their reintegration into mainstream society.

For these women, the decision to stop deviant behavior was preceded by a variety of factors. The majority of these factors revolved around social reactions to their behaviors. For instance, many of the women reported an increase in their formal contacts with the criminal justice system—increased arrests, informal dispositions, and even incarcerations. Other women reported increased difficulties in maintaining any sort of living arrangements, including the most basic shelter, food, and clothing. Yet for other women, the "final" threat of sanctions or complete withdrawal by family or close relations affected their decisions to desist. Most of the women also recalled a precipitous decline in their physical and mental health. A few stated that religious conversions or immersion into alternative sociocultural settings with powerful norms (e.g., treatment ideology) provided paths for cessation.

There were several processes that sustained and reinforced the changed behaviors on the part of those who decided to quit. For some, simple changes in physical location and social networks precipitated desistance. For others, transformations of identity and the formation of ties to conventional lifestyles aided them in easing out of the life. Yet several of the women reported that changes in the functional definitions of the problem behavior and displacement of the old behavior with new forms of behavior or expression (from religion, to physical outlets, to strong belief systems) were responsible for the transition. In this chapter we explore some of these factors with this subsample of women.

Resolving to Stop

Despite its initial excitement and allure, street life is hard. A host of severe personal problems plague most street offenders and normally become progressively worse as the careers continue. In our study, the women's lives were dominated by a powerful, often incapacitating, need for drugs. Consequently, economic problems were the most frequent complaint voiced by the respondents. Savings were quickly exhausted, and the culture of addiction justified the use of virtually any means to get money in order to support their habits.

For the majority of women, the problem of maintaining an addiction took precedence over all other interests and over participation in other social worlds. Their primary reference group—people they associated with—was involved in a wide range of illicit behaviors. Over time, the study women became further enmeshed in deviance and further alienated, both socially and psychologically, from conventional life. The women's lives became bereft of conventional involvements, obligations, and responsibilities. The excitement of the lifestyle that may have characterized their early criminal career phase gave way to a much more serious and grave daily existence.

The following accounts illustrate the uncertainty and vulnerability of street life. Denise, a 33-year-old black woman, participated in a wide range of street crimes including burglary, robbery, assault, and drug dealing. She began dealing drugs when she was 14 and used cocaine on a regular basis by the age of 19.

> I was in a lot of fights. So I had fights over, uh, drugs, or, you know, just manipulation. There's a lot of manipulation in that life. Everybody's tryin' to get over. Everybody will stab you in your back, you know. Nobody gives a fuck about the next person, you know. It's just when you want it, you want it. You know, when you want that drug, you know, you want that drug. There's a lot of lyin', a lot of manipulation. It's, it's, it's crazy! It also got frightening.

Gazella, a 38-year-old Hispanic woman, had been involved in crime for 22 years when we interviewed her:

> I'm 34 years old. I ain't no young woman no more, man. Drugs have changed, lifestyles have changed. Kids are killing you now for turf. Yeah, turf, and I was destroyin' myself. I was miserable. I was . . . I was gettin' high all the time to stay up to keep the business going, and it was really nobody I could trust. Things kept getting worse and worse. Everything was spoiling around me.

Sonya, a 27-year-old Hispanic woman, provides an account of what daily life was like on the streets:

> You get tired of bein' tired, you know. I got tired of hustlin', you know. I got tired of livin' the way I was livin', you know. Due to your body, your body, mentally, emotionally, you know. Everybody's tryin' to get over. Everybody will stab you in your back. Nobody gives a fuck about the next person. And I used to have people talkin' to me, "You know, you're not a bad lookin' girl. You know, why you don't get yourself together?"

Additional illustrations of the exigencies of street life are provided by April and Stephanie. April was a 25-year-old black woman at the time of the interview who had been involved in crime since she was 11:

I wasn't eating. Sometimes I wouldn't eat for 2 or 3 days. And I would . . . a lot of times I wouldn't have the time, or I wouldn't want to spend the money to eat—I've got to use it to get high. My teeth were falling out, and I looked real bad. I never knew what was going to happen next—whether I would have something to eat, someplace to live, anything.

Stephanie, a 27-year-old black woman, had used and sold crack for 5 years:

I knew that, uh, I was gonna get killed out here. I wasn't havin' no respect for myself. No one else was respecting me. Every relationship I got into, as long as I did drugs, it was gonna be constant disrespect involved, and it come . . . to the point of me gettin' killed. I had a few times when I thought that was going to happen—that that was going to be the end of it.

When the "spiral down" finally reached its lowest point, the women reported being overwhelmed by a sense of personal despair. In reporting the early stages of this period of despair, the respondents consistently voiced two themes: the hopeless futility of their lives and their personal isolation. Barbara, a 31-year-old black woman, began using crack when she was 23. By age 25, Barbara had lost her job at the Board of Education and was involved in burglary and robbery. Her account is typical of the despair the women in our sample eventually experienced:

The fact that my family didn't trust me anymore, and the way that my daughter was looking at me, and, uh, my mother wouldn't let me in her house anymore, and I was sleepin' on the trains. And I was sleepin' on the beaches in the summertime. And I was really frightened. I was real scared of the fact that I had to sleep on the train. And, uh, I had to wash up in the Port Authority. I was alone and no one was helping me anymore. I used to have my family when things got real rough. I always thought I would eventually have my daughter. But I was all of a sudden, all alone.

The effects of the spiral down were also felt by Gazella, who was forced to live on the streets:

It was the first time that I didn't have a place to live. My kids had been taken away from me. You know, constantly being harassed like 3 days out of the week by the Tactical Narcotics Team (police). I didn't want to be bothered with people. I was gettin' tired of the lyin', schemin', you know, stayin' in abandoned buildings, runnin', hidin', and all the while looking for more drugs. It was the final thing of living on the streets and all that came with it that did me in. There was no future.

For many of the women, it was the stresses of street life and the fear of dying on the streets that motivated their decision to quit the criminal life. Darlene, a 25-year-old black woman, recalled the stress associated with the latter stage of her drug selling career:

The simple fact is that I really, I thought that I would die out there. I thought that someone would kill me out there and I would be killed. I had a fear of being on the front page one day and being in the newspaper dying. I wanted to live, and I didn't just want to exist. But the street didn't let me do either, really. It got to the point where I wasn't even sure that I existed.

Alicia, a 29-year-old Hispanic woman, became involved in street violence when she was 12 years old. She comments on the personal isolation that was a consequence of her involvement in crime. In her case, though, the estrangement came from her end:

When I started getting involved in crime, you know, and drugs, the friends that I had, even my family, I stayed away from them, you know. You know how you look bad and you feel bad, and you just don't want those people to see you like you are. So I avoided seeing them. I didn't want them seeing me that way or knowing how low I got to get the drugs. But things got real bad on the street. I was totally out there alone. I stopped knowing who I was, really. What happened to the me who had a family?

For some, the emotional depth of the rock-bottom crisis was felt as a sense of mortification. Here, the women felt they had nowhere to turn to salvage a sense of well-being or self-worth. Suicide was considered a better alternative than remaining in such an undesirable social and psychological state. Denise's account was typical of the women who had attempted suicide as a way out of the life:

I ran into a girl who I went to school with that works on Wall Street. And I compared her life to mine and it was like miserable. Here she had a family, a job, friends. She looked good. She cared about herself. She had people who cared about her. It made me just want out. I was tired, I was run down, looking bad. I thought I could get out, forever, by smashing myself through a sixth-floor window. But I lived. Then I went to the psychiatric ward and I met this real nice doctor, and we talked every day. She fought to keep me in the hospital because she felt I wouldn't survive. She believed in me. And she talked me into going into a drug program.

Marginalization from family, friends, children, legal work—in short, the loss of traditional life structures—left women like Denise feeling hypervulnerable to chaotic street conditions. But for the women in this desistance subsample, the overwhelming sense of despair that had overcome them also led them, eventually, to begin the process of questioning and reevaluating their identities and their social construction of the world.

The women we spoke to repeated over and over that they had grown tired of a life filled with constant pain, terror, distress, and severe hardship. Even incarceration came to be viewed as yet another assault, rather than a respite, as some had believed earlier. The bottom line was that they grew tired of the street experiences and the problems and consequences of criminal involvement. This has been an observation commonly made by researchers on male offenders (Cusson and Pinsonneault, 1986; Shover, 1985). It appears as though, regardless of gender, with age the prospect of incurring another prison term becomes more difficult to deal with and affects decisions to desist.

Gazella recalls her last prison term:

First of all when I was in prison I was like, I was so humiliated. At my age [38] I was really kind of embarrassed, but I knew that was the lifestyle that I was leadin'. And people I used to talk to would tell me well you could do this, and you don't have to get busted. But then I started thinking why are all these people here. So it doesn't, you know, really work. So I came home, and I did go back to selling again, but you know I knew I was on probation. And I didn't want to do no more time. I knew that I wasn't going to survive the next time. I couldn't handle the thought of doing time again.

April, too, grew tired of being confined and anticipated with dread the potential for subsequent incarceration:

Jail, being in jail. The environment, having my freedom taken away. I saw myself keep repeating the same pattern, and I didn't want to do that. Uh, I had missed my daughter. See, being in jail that long period of time, I was able to detox. And when I detoxed, I kind of like had a clear sense of thinking, and that's when I came to the realization that, uh, this is not working for me. It used to be a place to rest, but the last time was too tough. I felt like I was climbing the walls—that I would never get out alive. If I stayed in this life, I would have ended up again in jail. But I wouldn't make it out next time. Oh God, I know I couldn't do it again.

Denise had never been incarcerated, but the prospect of it frightened her in a way that she never had thought about in the past:

Oh yeah, people were always going away. Maybe my turn would come one day. That's what I used to think. Then I saw the person that I was dealing with—my partner—I saw her go upstate to Bedford for 2 to 4 years. I didn't want to deal with it. I didn't want to go. Bedford is a prison, women's prison. And I couldn't see myself givin' up 2 years of my life for something that I knew I could change in another way. I knew it wasn't too late for me and that my luck was probably going to be running out soon too. Never thought about it that way before, but I really am scared of spending the next few years of my life living like my partner.

As we can see, a change in these women's attitude toward surviving incarceration (which they increasingly viewed as a realistic outcome of their continued involvement in criminal behavior) affected their decisions to desist.

Perhaps even more important, the women felt that they had wasted time. They became acutely aware of time as a diminishing resource (Shover, 1983). The women reported that they saw themselves going nowhere and that they did not have much more time to get on with things. The women arrived at a point at which crime seemed senseless and their lives had reached a dead end. Implicit in this assessment was the belief that gaining a longer range perspective on one's life was a first step in changing. These deliberations developed as a result of "socially disjunctive experiences" that caused the women to experience social stress, feelings of alienation, and dissatisfaction with their present identities (Ray, 1961).

Breaking Away from the Life

Forming a commitment to change was only the first step taken by these women toward ending their criminal careers. The women then entered a period that has been characterized as a "running struggle" with problems of social identity (Ray, 1961:136). To be successful at desistance, these women had to work hard at clarifying and strengthening their nondeviant identity and at redefining their street experiences in terms more compatible with conventional lifestyles. This second stage of desistance required that the woman make a public announcement or "certification" (Meisenhelder, 1977:329) that she had decided to end her criminal involvement. Once accomplished, she then had to begin to redefine the economic, social, and emotional relationships that had been rooted in the deviant street subculture.

This period was one of ambivalence and crisis. For these women, so much of their lives had revolved around street life. Further, they had, at best, only weak associations with the conventional world. Many of the women remembered the uncertainty they felt and the social dilemmas they faced after they decided to stop their involvement in crime. Denise describes her own situation:

I went and looked up my old friends and to see what was doing, and my girlfriend Mia was like, she was gettin' paid. And I was livin' on a $60 stipend. And I wasn't with it. Mia was good to me, she always kept money in my pocket when I came home. I would walk into her closet and change into clothes that I'm more accustomed to. She started calling me Pen again. She stopped calling me Denise. And I would ride with her knowing that she had a gun or a package in the car. But I wouldn't touch nothin'. But that was my rationale. As long as I don't fuck with nothin'. Yeah, she was like I can give you a grand and get you started. I said I know you can, but I can't. She said I can give you a grand, and she kept telling me that over and over; and I wasn't that far from taking the grand and getting started again. I was confused for a while and it caused me lots of pain.

Barbara also offered an account of her experiences:

After I decided to change, I went to a party with my friend. And people was around me and they was drinkin' and stuff, and I didn't want to drink. I don't have the urge of drinking. If anything, it would be smokin' crack. And when I left the party, I felt like I was missing something—like something was missing. And it was the fact that I wasn't gettin' high. But I know the consequences of it. If I take a drink, I'm gonna smoke crack. If I, uh, sniff some blow, I'm gonna smoke crack. I might do some things like rob a store or something stupid and go to jail. So I don't want to put myself in that position. But it really hurt to not be down with them.

At this stage of their transition, the women had to face some very basic issues. Perhaps foremost was the dilemma about what to do with themselves and their lives. Furthermore, they were clueless in terms of how to establish and maintain conventional relationships. Few of the women had maintained their ties to people who were not involved in crime and drugs. And given their family histories, few had past experiences from which to model. Given this situation, the women had to work hard in order to construct alternatives to their deviant social worlds.

The large majority of the women were aided in their social reintegration by help that was outside of their social worlds. The women perceived clearly the need to remove themselves from the "scene," to meet new friends and to begin the process of identity reformation. Often, they sought formal treatment of some kind as a way of removing themselves from the ever-present and overpowerful deviant social world. Typically, they entered residential drug treatment programs that provided them with structure, social support, and a pathway to behavioral change. The following account by Alicia typifies the importance of a "geographic cure."

> I love to get high. You know, and I love the way crack makes me feel. I knew that I needed long-term, I knew that I needed to go somewhere. All away from everything, and I just needed to be away from everything. And I couldn't deal with responsibility at all. And, uh, I was just so ashamed of the way that I had, you know, became and the person that I became that I just wanted to start over again. But it wasn't going to happen if I stayed in the same place. I had to get away from the pull.

Social avoidance strategies were a common thread in all of their attempts at desistance. Clearly, they recognized that their continued involvement in crime and drugs would be made more difficult if they removed themselves from their old social worlds and old locations. April discussed this issue with us:

> Yeah, I go home, but I don't, I don't socialize with the people. I don't even speak to anybody really. I go and I come. I don't go to the areas

that I used to be in. I don't go there anymore. I don't walk down the same blocks I used to walk down. I always take different locations. I avoid those people and sometimes, I know that I can't even go home if I am feeling weak. I need that space away from those influences. Anyway, they'll forget about me if I'm not around, and I'll lose those connections if I stay away long enough. That's what I have to do to stay out of the life.

Denise, too, acknowledges the importance of maintaining distance from her old world:

I miss the fast money; otherwise I don't miss my old life. I get support from my positive friends, and in the program. I talk about how I felt being around my old associates, seeing them, you know, going back to my old neighborhood. It's hard to deal with, I have to push away. I have to stay away. That way, I can keep strong and give up on the fast money. Being away helps me remember how low I got and how the fast money didn't buy me a life. As long as I stay away, I can keep clear of those things.

Maintaining a Conventional Life

Most of these women have little chance of staying "out of the life" for an extended period of time if they stay in the social world of crime and addiction. Instead, they must build and *maintain* a network of primary relations who accept and support their nondeviant identity. This third stage of desistance is essential if they are to be successful. Surely, this is no easy task. Desisters have in most cases alienated their old, nondeviant primary relations.

But these women worked hard at maintaining the straight and narrow. They were like religious converts in terms of the fervor with which they attempted to establish and maintain support networks that validated their new sense of self. This was facilitated by their participation in treatment programs.

Generally, treatment programs provide not only a ready-made primary group for the desister, but also a well-established *pervasive identity* (Travisano, 1970). Thus, being an ex-con and/or an ex-addict continually informed the woman's view of herself in a variety of interactions. Reminders of "spoiled identities" (Goffman, 1963) such as criminal, ex-con, and ex-junkie serve as constant reference points for new experiences. Further, they help maintain the saliency of conventional living (Faupel, 1991). Perhaps most important in terms of treatment programs is the simple fact that they provided the women with an alternative basis for life structure, one that was devoid of crime, drugs, and other subcultural elements.

The successful treatment program, however, is one that ultimately facilitates dissociation and promotes independent living. Dissociation from programs to participate in conventional living requires association or reintegration with conventional society. For the study women, friends and educational and occupational roles developed within the context of these treatment programs helped to reaffirm their noncriminal identities and bond them to conventional lifestyles. Barbara describes the assistance she received from friends and from her treatment groups:

> The program has given me a bunch of friends that always confronts me on what I'm doin' and where I'm goin', and they just want the best for me. And none of them use drugs. I go to a lot like outside support groups, you know. They help me have more confidence in myself. I have new friends now. Some of them are in treatment. Some have always been straight. They know. You know, they glad, you know, when I see them. They're always there for me, and I'm learning to be there for them. I feel like I belong, that there is a place for me with them. It is really great that straight people even accept me.

In the course of experiencing relationships with conventional others and participating in conventional roles, the women developed a strong social-psychological commitment not to return to crime and drug use. These commitments were often strengthened by renewed affiliations with their children, relationships with new friends, and the acquisition of educational and vocational skills.

The social relationships, interests, and investments that developed in the course of desistance reflected the gradual emergence of their new identities. Such stakes in conventional identity form the social-psychological context within which control and desistance were possible (Waldorf et al., 1991). In short, the women developed a stake in their new lives that was incompatible with street life. These new stakes served as wedges to help maintain the separation of the women from the world of the streets (Biernacki, 1986).

This desire to maintain one's sense of self was an important incentive for avoiding return to crime. As Alicia recounts:

I like the fact that I have my respect back. I like the fact that, uh, my daughter trusts me again. And my mother don't mind leavin' me in the house, and she don't have to worry that when she come in her TV might be gone. I feel real good about this.

Barbara, too, takes great pride in her new self identify:

I have new friends. I have my children back in my life. I have my education. It keeps me straight. I can't forget where I came from because I get scared to go back. I don't want to go back. I don't want to hurt nobody. I just want to live a normal life. It has been tough, but look what I have in return—my family, great friends who love me for who I really am, a future. It was a long road, but I'm not turning back.

But for some, the tension between staying straight and returning to the deviant street scene is tremendous. Janelle, a 22-year-old black woman, started dealing drugs and carrying a .38-caliber gun when she was 15. She describes this ongoing tension:

It's hard, it's hard stayin' on the right track. But lettin' myself know that I'm worth more helps. I don't have to go in a store today and steal anything. I don't deserve that. I don't deserve to make myself feel really bad. Then once again I would be steppin' back and feel that this is all I can do. I feel like I'm being pulled between these two worlds and I am not sure where I will fit in. I guess it will all depend on what's comfortable.

Overall, the way to an identity transformation hinged on the women's abilities to establish and maintain commitments and involvements in conventional aspects of life. As the women began to feel accepted and trusted within some conventional social circles, their determination to exit from crime was strengthened, as were their social and personal identities as noncriminals. Their "comfort" with their new identities was crucial to maintaining the desistance process.

The Desistance Process

Desistance is a process as complex and lengthy as the processes of initial involvement. It was interesting to find that some of the key concepts in initiation of deviance—social bonding, differential association, deterrence, age—were equally important in the process of desistance. We see the aging offender take the threat of punishment seriously, reestablish links with conventional society, and sever associations with subcultural street elements.

We found, too, that the decision to give up crime was triggered by a shock of some sort that was followed by a period of crisis. Anxious and dissatisfied, the women took stock of their lives and criminal activity. They arrived at a point at which the deviant way of life seemed senseless. Having made this assessment, the women then worked to clarify and strengthen their nondeviant identities. This phase began with the reevaluation of life goals and the public announcement of their decision to end their involvement in crime. Once the decision to quit was made, the women turned to (or created new) relationships that had not been ruined by their deviance. The final stage, maintaining cessation, involved integration into a nondeviant lifestyle. This meant restructuring the entire pattern of their lives (i.e., primary relationships, daily routines, social situations). For most women, treatment groups provided the continuing support to maintain a nondeviant status.

The change processes and turning points described by the women were quite similar to those reported by men in previous studies (Shover, 1983, 1985; Cusson and Pinsonneault, 1986). Basically, turning points occur as a "part of a process over time and not as a dramatic lasting change that takes place at any one time" (Pickles and Rutter, 1991:134). Thus, the return to conventional life occurs more because of "push" rather than "pull" factors (Adler, 1992). This appears to result from a point of time in the criminal career when involvement in crime moves offenders beyond the point at which she or he finds it enjoyable to the point at which it is debilitating and anxiety provoking.

Clearly, these interviews are limited in terms of their generalizability. Yet there are some important ideas that emerged from this group of women who were deeply involved in crime and immersed in a street subculture but found the strength and resources to change their lives. At the same time, the fact that all of the women who quit their involvement in crime experienced a long period of personal deterioration and a "rock-bottom" experience before they were able to exit does not mean that all who hit that point will stop or that this is the only process by which offenders will desist. There are undoubtedly other scenarios. There is always the case of the occasional offender who will forever drift in and out of crime; there is the offender who stops when criminal involvement threatens and conflicts with commitments to conventional life; and there is the battered woman who kills only once, in response to her abusive situation; in this instance, the question of desistance does not arise.

Nevertheless, the experiences of these women offer useful perspectives for thinking about a theory of cessation. Drawing on their accounts as well as on common themes in the literature on exiting or "quitting" deviant careers, we present a model for understanding desistance from crime (Figure 6.1). Three stages characterize the cessation process: recognition of problems associated with criminal participation (e.g., socially disjunctive experiences), restructuring of the self, and maintenance of the new behaviors and integration into new social networks (Stall and Biernacki, 1986; Mulvey and Aber, 1988). These phases resemble the cessation processes described by Waldorf et al. (1991:240) in their study of cocaine quitters. They described three ideal-typical phases of desistance: "turning points," when offenders begin consciously to experience negative effects (socially disjunctive experiences); "active quitting," when they take steps to exit crime (public pronouncement); and "maintaining cessation" (identity transformation).

Stage 1: Catalysts for Change

When external conditions change and reduce the "rewards of deviant behavior," motivation may build to end criminal involvement. That process and the resulting decision seem to be associated with two related conditions: (1) a series of negative, aversive, unpleasant experiences from criminal behavior and (2) corollary situations in which the positive rewards, status, or gratifications from crime are reduced. Shover and Thompson's (1992) research suggested that the probability of desistance from criminal participation increases as expectations for achieving rewards (e.g., friends, money, autonomy) via crime decrease and that changes in expectations are age-related.

Shover (1983) contended that the daily routines of managing criminal involvement become tiring and burdensome to aging of-

FIGURE 6.1   The Desistance Process

Stage 1   Problems associated with criminal participation

Socially Disjunctive Experiences	*Delayed Deterrence*
Hitting rock bottom	Increased probability of punishment
Fear of death	Increased difficulty in "doing time"
Tiredness	Increased severity of sanctions
Illness	Increasing fear

Assessment
Reappraisal of life and goals
Psychic change

Decision
Decision to quit or initial attempts at desistance
Continuing possibility of criminal participation

Stage 2   Restructuring of self

Public pronouncement of decision to end criminal participation
Claim to a new social identity

Stage 3   Maintenance of the decision to stop

Ability to successfully renegotiate identity
Support of significant others
Integration into new social networks
Ties to conventional roles
Stabilization of new social identity

fenders. Consequently, the allure of crime diminishes as offenders get older. Aging may also increase the perceived formal risk of criminal participation. Cusson and Pinsonneault (1986:76) pointed out that "with age, criminals raise their estimates of the certainty of punishment." Fear of reimprisonment, fear of longer sentences, and the increasing difficulty of "doing time" have often been reported by investigators who have explored desistance.

Stage 2: Discontinuance

The second stage of the model begins with the public announcement that the offender has decided to end her criminal participation. Such an announcement forces the start of a process of renegotiation of the offender's social identity (Stall and Biernacki, 1986).

After this announcement, the offender must not only cope with the instrumental aspects (e.g., financial) of her life but also begin to redefine important emotional and social relationships that are influenced or predicated upon criminal behavior.

Leaving a deviant subculture is difficult. Biernacki (1986) noted the exclusiveness of the social involvements maintained by former addicts during initial stages of abstinence. With social embedment comes the gratification of social acceptance and social identity. The decision to end a behavior that is socially determined and supported implies withdrawal of the social gratification it brings. Thus, the more deeply embedded in a criminal social context, the more dependent the offender is on that social world for her primary sources of approval and social definition.

The responses by social control agents, family members, and peer supporters to further criminal participation are critical to shaping the outcome of discontinuance. New social and emotional worlds to replace the old ones may strengthen the decision to stop. Adler (1992) found that outside associations and involvements provided a critical bridge back into society for dealers who decided to leave the drug subculture. With discontinuance comes the difficult work of identity transformations (Biernacki, 1986) and establishing new social definitions of behavior and relationships to reinforce them.

Stage 3: Maintenance

Following the initial stages of discontinuance, strategies to avoid a return to crime build on the initial strategies to break from a lengthy pattern of criminal participation: further integration into a noncriminal identity and social world and maintaining the costs of criminal participation. Maintenance depends in part on replacing deviant networks of peers and associates with supports that both sanction criminal participation and approve of new, nondeviant beliefs. Treatment interventions (e.g., drug treatment, social service programs) are important sources of alternative social supports to maintain a noncriminal lifestyle. In other words, maintenance depends on immersion into a social world in which criminal behavior meets immediately with strong formal and informal sanctions. Despite these efforts to maintain noncriminal involvement, desistance is likely to be episodic, with occasional bouts interspersed with lengthening of lulls.

Cessation is part of a social-psychological transformation for the offender. A strategy to stabilize the transition to a noncriminal lifestyle requires the active use of supports to maintain the norms that have been substituted for the forces that supported criminal behavior in the past.

Notes

1. A problematic aspect of the definition of desistance is its permanence. Termination that is followed by criminal involvement might be considered "false" (Blumstein et al., 1985). Elliott et al. (1989) have avoided the variable termination by using the variable suspension, a temporary or permanent cessation of criminal activity during a particular period of time. Clearly, we cannot know if the study women have demonstrated "true desistance." The data presented here do not warrant the conclusion that none of the women ever renewed their involvement in crime. That the study materials consisted of retrospective information with all its attendant problems precludes stating with certainty whether desistance from crime is permanent. Still, it also is clear that these women broke their pattern of involvement in crime for substantial lengths of time and have changed their lives. A 2-year hiatus from crime certainly indicates temporary cessation, and more important, it is a long enough period of time to consider the processes that initiate and sustain desistance.

Chapter Seven

Breaking with the Past: Challenging Assumptions About Women and Violent Crime

Gender, Crime, and Neighborhood Decline

What we have drawn in the preceding chapters is a portrait of the lives of women involved in street violence. We have tried to depict their subjective realities in terms comprehensible to those who have not experienced deviant street subcultures. We have incorporated the link between childhood and adult deviance, emphasizing a cumulative, developmental process wherein delinquent behavior attenuates the social and institutional bonds linking adults to society. Although we do not deny the reality of individual decision making or that persons may sometimes "create" their own environment (Laub and Sampson, 1993), our focus has been on the role of structural dislocation, community context, and opportunity structure in shaping the life course. We have explored how personal decisions related to participation in violent crimes are mediated by the women's experiences and understandings of their immediate environments. The analyses presented here do not imply that the women had no choice or attempt to absolve the women from responsibility for their actions but claim only to indicate that, under certain conditions and in certain contexts, some women are more likely than not to choose to be involved in violent crime.

Our analysis of the factors and developmental processes involved in female violent offending leads us to two important ob-
servations. First, our research has produced results that clearly
challenge contemporary assumptions regarding female offending.
Our analysis suggests a complex relationship that serves as a cau-
tion against generic and gender-based generalizations that have
been drawn from time-bound, aggregate-level data sets and from
ethnographies of women's involvement in street hustling. The
findings of this book suggest that an adequate understanding of female offending must consider the impact of neighborhood, peer,
and addiction factors that affect both male and female participation in criminal violence. In addition, it appears as though different
configurations of these factors contribute to the initiation of violent
offending depending on the age of onset.

It is essential to note that these findings as well as their interpretation are suggestive and require further validation with a more
geographically diverse and larger sample. Nonetheless, the findings do lend support to theoretical and substantive explanations
that emerge from an integrated perspective. The convergence of
social learning, control, and ecological theories helps to explain
how weak school attachments and parental supervision, associations with delinquent peers, as well as other social and economic
processes (e.g., relative deprivation, increased opportunities for illegal activities, fewer conventional role models) prevalent in severely distressed communities combined with individual-level
and situational factors to initiate involvement in violent street
crime for the 170 women who participated in our study.

Nonetheless, the results suggest variation among the study
women. The findings demonstrate that individual-level factors related to onset of violent crime patterns change as youths age
through adolescence. On the one hand, early initiation into violent
crime was accompanied by participation in a wide variety of other
offending behaviors and deviant lifestyles. On the other hand,
women who experienced a later onset of violent offending did so
within the context of a criminal career that, up to the point of substance abuse, was more specialized and focused on typically nonviolent, gender-congruent activities (e.g., prostitution, shoplifting).
Therefore, in terms of prevention and control, criminal justice policies and practices need to be geared toward the particularities of

these two career paths in terms of timing, content, and breadth of intervention.

Second, the data examined in this book reaffirm the importance of social factors in accounting for violent career patterns. The results suggest that initiation into violent street crime for the 170 study women was strongly influenced by the neighborhood environment. These women came from the most severely distressed communities in New York City, where the stresses of poverty and the increases in illegal opportunities combined with a weakening in the social control capabilities of neighborhood institutions. Thus, these women grew up in multiproblem households where the absence of conventional role models, social support, and material resources weakened the socialization functions of the family. They experienced detachment from such conventional institutions as school, marriage, and employment, and by adulthood, most were deeply entrenched in substance abuse and related deviant lifestyles.

In short, the women in our study operated within a "daily-life environment" that closed into a prison of space and resources. Deficiencies in their neighborhoods—limitations on mobility and the density and quality of social resources–clearly limited their potential, or their market capacity, and similarly, their access to more favorable environments.

The heightened insecurity that economic crisis has brought to American life—the receding prospects for decent jobs and decent housing, the looming threat of downward mobility and of an impoverished adulthood—helps explain the resurgence of broader cultural themes of competition and individual survival. It encourages the desperate focus on the "self," the "me first," "I don't give a shit" character of life lived mainly in the present because the future seems less and less certain or worth building toward. The women in our study accept this fate; they live on the edge. Their manner conveys the message that nothing matters and nothing intimidates them.

The growing concentration of poverty, joblessness, and family disruption has signaled a transformation in the social and institutional structure of the inner city. In turn, there has been a general weakening in the structures of economic opportunities and processes of social sanctions that mediate the development of social and economic capital for inner-city residents. Neighborhood change has weakened formal and informal social controls, and the material and social rewards for legal behavior have all but disappeared. In this milieu, young people in inner cities have become involved in a variety of serious and potentially lethal criminal activities. And this involvement reached unprecedented numbers in the 1980s.

Our research suggests that these processes, so often identified as criminogenic in terms of inner-city males, affect women living in these communities, as well. For both men and women in a changing economy, filling the market niche for drug products or other illegal goods is a logical entrepreneurial response, particularly when the historical avenues to labor-market participation have been truncated by the restructuring of the city and regional economy. The informal economy grew disproportionately in the 1980s in New York neighborhoods with high concentrations of poor, minority populations (Sassen-Koob, 1989), and drug selling has always been an important part of the informal economy (Fagan, 1992). The growth in drug use and the rapid expansion of the cocaine and crack markets in the 1980s created a complex drug industry, albeit one that functioned outside formal (legal) systems of regulation and that relied on violence for its maintenance (Goldstein, 1989)[1]. Drawn by the promise of high profits with minimal capital investment, drug sellers became suppliers of important goods and services to both local markets and residents of more affluent areas (Sullivan, 1989). Thus, the vitality of a drug market in a neighborhood is bound up with the relationships within poor neighborhoods and between these neighborhoods and other parts of their cities. To the extent that women's roles and prominence have changed in transformed neighborhoods, women's involvement in drug selling and other crimes that include street violence reflects the dynamics of the neighborhoods themselves.

A Rational Policy

The societal response to crime problems, which itself arises from social and economic conditions, has been the traditional crackdown, rooted in deterrence and punishment theories. The anti-crime crusades of the 1980s have translated into laws and policies that rely heavily on criminal sanctions, especially incarceration.[2] Sentences for drug offenders in New York City in the 1980s reflected ideological trends that regard punishment as both symbolic and substantive components of antidrug sentiment (Fagan, 1994). The enactment and popularization of laws mandating incarceration, regardless of their enforcement, symbolized public contempt for both users and sellers (Myers, 1989), whereas the mobilization of legal institutions to punish drug offenders reflected public will to wage "war" against drug users.

Whatever the successes of the symbolic component of crime control policy, its specific deterrent effects evidently are quite limited for certain subgroups of offenders, especially for those who were involved in the large and active drug market in New York in the 1980s. For both male and female crack arrestees in 1986, prison sentences were as likely as probation terms, regardless of the defendant's prior record or severity of the drug offense (Belenko, Fagan, and Chin, 1991). The sentences were ineffective, too. Recidivism for either a drug or a violent offense was as likely to occur among drug offenders sentenced to prison as among those placed on probation (Fagan, 1994). The same results might easily be achieved by chance. The limited effects of incarceration for all types of drug offenders call into question the fairness and validity of mandatory prison sentences for drug offenders.

The cost of the societal policy falls most heavily on communities already burdened by the deterioration of local economies, the flight of economic opportunities from the surrounding region, and the expansion of drug markets and the violence that sustains them. These communities and their residents live with the effects of political and economic decisions over which they have little control. These decisions include not only the allocation and policies of legal institutions, but also decisions regarding schools, zoning, and local services. The results raise doubts about the implied econometric model of specific deterrence that does not consider nonlegal factors.

The exclusive focus on deterrence in the supply side of crime control policy discounts important factors that are part of the natural process of desistance from crime, drug use, and drug selling. This focus also discounts the economic context of decisions to persist or desist from crime. Mounting a specific deterrent effect in the face of widespread drug involvement, for example, may be an insurmountable challenge for legal institutions. The relocation of sentencing discretion from judges to the legislature, and in turn to prosecutors through their decisions regarding specific charges, has achieved a uniformity in sentencing that serves political goals but adds little to the deterrent effect of punishment. Can we reasonably expect to jail all drug offenders? The weak effects of punishment may have counterdeterrent effects that breed disrespect for the laws and institutions that the punishments are designed to uphold. The enforcement of ineffective laws undermines respect for legal institutions more generally, reinforcing the illicit economies and their influence on social controls within neighborhoods. The challenge for policy is to contribute to the processes that motivate offenders to stop. This requires a balanced policy that addresses both punishment for law violation and efforts to revalue the gains from legal behaviors.

The limited choices for punishment present an opportunity for balanced policy. The current reliance on the extremes of incarceration and probation offer little substantive choice for judges and policymakers. Instead of questioning the underlying assumptions of specific deterrence, our society responds to the limited effects of punishment with more serious punishment. A range of sanctions makes more sense. For offenders, interventions are needed that increase human capital—job skills and education—and that are part of the mix of pressures and escape paths that also characterize desistance from crime and drug use. Expanding the options for sentencing might restore a more rational allocation of punishments that recognizes the varying thresholds and reactivity of offenders to sanctions.

Finally, legal doctrines will be ineffective unless sanctions are accompanied by related policies that emphasize the conditions in which deterrence becomes effective, conditions that both provide and revalue legal opportunities for financial gain, increase the costs of illicit gain, and reduce the opportunities for crime. That these concerns apply equally to men and women attests to the new dynamics of crime in which gender is a far less salient factor.

Notes

1. The markets themselves reflected differences in the types of drugs and their psychoactive effects: Compared to heroin and marijuana street sales, cocaine and crack markets were more volatile owing to the high

rate of transactions and the short half-life of the high they produced (Bourgois, 1989; Hamid, 1990; Johnson, Hamid, and Morales, 1990).

2. Between 1980 and 1994, the number of women incarcerated in state and federal prisons increased by 387 percent. The increased number of women imprisoned is the result primarily of legislative responses to the "war on drugs." Nationwide, between 1983 and 1992, the number of women arrested for drug violations increased by 84.7 percent, whereas the number of men arrested for such charges increased by 53 percent (Federal Bureau of Investigation, 1993). Further, a nationwide survey of state prison inmates in 1991 revealed that females were more likely than their male counterparts to have used drugs in the month before the offense (54 vs. 50 percent) and to have been under the influence at the time of the offense (36 vs. 31 percent; Bureau of Justice Statistics, 1996). Also, nearly 1 in 4 women in prison reported having committed their crimes to obtain money for drugs, compared to about 1 in 6 men (Bureau of Justice Statistics, 1996).

Appendix:
Research Methods and Sample Description

Location of the Sample

Our research was based primarily on in-depth, life history interviews with 170 women who committed nondomestic violent felony crimes (robbery, assault, homicide) in New York City. The women were recruited from various social settings and included (1) those arrested and arraigned for violent crimes, (2) those in state prison for violent crimes, and (3) women actively involved in violent criminal offending.

Women currently involved in violent crime were recruited through arrangements with field-workers active in ethnographic research in Central Harlem, Washington Heights, and Bushwick (1992–1994). These ongoing studies were designed to collect data on drug sales and distribution, drug use, and nondrug criminality. Although these projects did not focus specifically on female violent crime, they established a strong field presence that provided fairly easy access to nonarrested neighborhood female offenders. Forty-three percent ($N = 73$) of the interviews were conducted with active offenders.

The sample contains 49 women arrested for nondomestic violent felony crimes (29 percent of the sample). Arraignment calendars for the time period between January and June 1990 were used in order to obtain a sample of women arrested for a violent felony offense. Access to complete court records permitted us to weed out those women whose arrests were related directly to domestic violence. Official data were collected on 176 women, and letters inviting participation in the study were sent to all women for whom there was a recent address ($N = 124$). Thirty letters were returned

as undeliverable (incorrect addresses, resident moved), and 49
women contacted us and completed interviews.

In addition to the community-based sample, New York State Department of Correctional Services databases were consulted in order to draw a similar incarceration sample. Women who had been
committed (to Bedford Hills and Bayview Correctional Facilities)
for a felony offense (murder/manslaughter, assault, robbery,
weapons possession, weapons use, burglary, arson, kidnapping)
during 1990 were eligible for study participation. Women whose
violent acts were of a domestic nature were excluded from the incarceration sample. Official records data were collected on 93 incarcerated women who fit study criteria. Forty-eight women
agreed to be interviewed (28 percent of the sample).

For the women residing in the community, interviews were conducted in a neutral location such as a library or a private office in a
university. In order to convey the neutrality and anonymity of the
study, we avoided offices of either criminal justice agencies or clin-
ical settings. The women were given a generous travel allowance
($10), regardless of the length or duration of their trip. A stipend of
$30 for the interview was paid at the conclusion of the interview,
although it was not contingent on completion of the interview. For
women who were incarcerated, interviews were conducted in a
private office within the correctional facility. These women did not
receive a stipend owing to institutional rules.

Interviews were open-ended, in-depth, and when possible, au-
diotaped. The open-ended technique created a context in which respondents were able to speak freely and in their own words. Furthermore, it facilitated the pursuit of issues that were raised by the
women during the interview but were not recognized beforehand
by the researchers. The in-depth interview approach enabled us to
pursue information about specific events, as well as to provide an
opportunity for respondents to reflect on those events. As a result,
we were able to gain insight into the women's attitudes, feelings,
and other subjective orientations to their experiences.

Time reference points were used to assist in the recall of information. The method of sequencing the interview into intervals that
are meaningful to the respondent has proved quite successful in
collecting retrospective, longitudinal data covering long periods of
time. The procedure requires that the interviewer work closely

with the respondent to structure the period of interest, using corroborative information and memory aids (e.g., life events and associated dates from official records). In this way, criminal behavior patterns and displacement, shifts in the frequency or severity of criminal involvement (lulls, episodes, relapses after lengthy desistance periods), and contributing situational factors (peer group roles, legal or social sanctions, and life events such as the birth of a child or loss of a job) can be temporally anchored over a multiyear period to establish the natural history of criminal behavior and the factors that have affected its course.

Obtaining an independent means to test the validity of at least some portion of the self-report data is particularly desirable for a study of this nature because the information to be collected could easily be subject to exaggeration or lack of recall. In the present research, estimates of individual offending patterns were confirmed independently through official arrest and conviction records. Official records data were used in the interview in order to help reduce response errors. Interviewers mentioned events found in the official record in order to trigger the recall of events and time periods as well as to curtail respondent misrepresentation of criminal activities.

Description of the Sample

As Table A.1 shows, a typical member of our sample is a black woman, 27 years old, a high school dropout with two children, possessing limited work experience. The youngest member of our sample was 16 years old and the oldest 43. The median age of our respondents was 30 years. Seventy-five percent of our subjects were high school dropouts, typically leaving school by eleventh grade. Although most of the women had worked in a legitimate job (80 percent), the median number of months employed was only 16, and the average was 35.9 months. Most of the women worked in unskilled and semiskilled working-class occupations (e.g., clerical and factory jobs).

Table A.1 shows self-reported lifetime prevalence of drug use, drug selling, and crime. The women reported that they were engaged in a wide range of criminal and deviant activities. Nearly all said they were experienced drug users. Seventy-two percent were

TABLE A.1   Demographic and Background Profile (*N* = 170)

Mean age	27.28
Race (%)	
White	2.9
Black	63.5
Hispanic	33.5
Mean years of school	10.27
School dropout (%)	75.0
Marital status (%)	
Married/living as married	6.5
Never married	70.6
Other	22.4
Children	
Have children (%)	83.0
Mean number	2.7
Employment history (%)	
Never worked	20.0
Workers (*N* = 136)	
Sales/cashier/food work	25.0
Clerical	32.0
Semiskilled (e.g., health aide)	15.0
Trade/factory	28.0
Problems while in school (%)	
(mean age of initiation)	
Fighting	67.0 (10.67)
Weapons possession	26.0 (12.33)
Truancy	89.0 (13.81)
Drugs	42.0 (14.48)
Family problems (%)	
Family member arrested	60.0
Family substance abuse	81.0
Family alcohol abuse	61.0
Family mental health problems	21.0

regular crack users, 49 percent used cocaine regularly, and 40 percent were at some point in time addicted to heroin.

Table A.2 shows lifetime participation rates and average initiation age in drug selling by drug type. Most (81 percent) of the women had sold crack. About half (52 percent and 45 percent) had sold heroin and cocaine, respectively. The mean age of initiation into dealing was before 25 years of age. Most had been selling for at least 5 years.

TABLE A.2 Drug Use, Drug Selling, and Crime History ($N = 170$)

	Drug Use History		
Drug	Ever Used (%)	Regular Use (%)	Mean Age of Initiation
Marijuana	95	45	15.02
Inhalants	18	1	14.37
Hallucinogens	36	2	17.79
PCP	36	1	19.04
Stimulants	19	6	18.76
Depressants	14	7	19.14
Cocaine	88	49	19.16
Crack	83	72	24.92
Heroin	55	40	20.86

	Dealing History		
Drug	Ever Dealt (%)	Mean Age of Initiation	Mean No. Months
Cocaine	69	23.55	64.68
Crack	81	25.79	42.24
Heroin	54	24.26	69.84
Marijuana	35	15.02	30.60
Other	12	24.39	61.12

	Crime History	
Offense	Ever Participated (%)	Mean Age of Initiation
Auto theft	19	19.40
Shoplifting	58	17.38
Forgery	29	22.24
Prostitution	40	23.23
Assault	58	20.86
Robbery	61	21.15
Burglary	17	24.52
Weapons possession	47	19.64

PCP = phencyclidine

References

Adler, Freda
1981   *The Incidence of Female Criminality in the Contemporary World.* New York: New York University Press.
1975   *Sisters in Crime: The Rise of the New Female Criminal.* New York: McGraw-Hill.
Adler, Freda, and Rita James Simon, eds.
1979   *The Criminology of Deviant Women.* Boston: Houghton Mifflin.
Adler, Patricia
1985   *Wheeling and Dealing: An Ethnography of an Upper-Level Dealing and Smuggling Community.* New York: Columbia University Press.
1992   The post phase of deviant careers: Reintegrating drug traffickers. *Deviant Behavior* 13:103–126.
Agnew, Robert
1991   The Interactive Effects of Peer Variables on Delinquency. *Criminology* 29:47–72.
Akers, Ronald, M. Krohn, L. Lanza-Kaduce, and M. Radosevich
1979   Social Learning and Deviant Behavior: A Specific Test of a General Theory. *American Sociological Review* 44:636–655.
Alexander, Priscilla
1987   Prostitutes Are Being Scapegoated for Heterosexual AIDS. In Frederique Delacoste and Priscilla Alexander (eds.), *Sexwork: Writings by Women in the Sex Industry.* San Francisco: Cleis: 248–263.
Alfaro, Jose
1981   Report on the Relationship Between Child Abuse and Neglect and Later Socially Deviant Behavior. In R. Hunner and Y. E. Walker (eds.), *Exploring the Relationships Between Child Abuse and Delinquency.* Montclair, NJ: Allanheld, Osmun.
1978   *Child Abuse and Subsequent Delinquent Behavior.* New York: Select Committee on Child Abuse.
Allan, E., and D. Steffensmeier
1989   Youth, Underemployment, and Property Crime: Differential Effects of Job Availability and Job Quality on Juvenile and Young Adult Arrest Rates. *American Sociological Review* 54:107–123.

Anderson, Elijah
1978   *A Place on the Corner.* Chicago: University of Chicago Press.
1990   *Streetwise.* Chicago: University of Chicago Press.
1994   The Code of the Streets. *The Atlantic Monthly*, May: 81–94.
Anderson, Linda, T. Chiricos, and G. Waldo
1977   Formal and Informal Sanctions: A Comparison of Deterrent Effects. *Social Problems* 25:103–112.
Arnold, R.
1990   Processes of Victimization and Criminalization of Black Women. *Social Justice* 17:153–166.
Austin, Roy
1982   Women's Liberation and Increases in Minor, Major and Occupational Offenses. *Criminology* 20:407–430.
Bachman, Jerald, S. Green, and I. Wirtanen
1971   Dropping Out: Problem or Symptom? *Youth in Transition, Vol. 3.* Ann Arbor, MI: Institute for Social Research.
Bachman, Jerald, and Patrick O'Malley
1978   *Youth in Transition, Volume VI: Adolescence to Adulthood: Change and Stability in the Lives of Young Men.* Ann Arbor, MI: University of Michigan Press.
Bachman, Jerald, P. O'Malley, and J. Johnston
1978   Adolescence to Adulthood: Change and Stability in the Lives of Young Men. *Youth in Transition, Vol. 6.* Ann Arbor, MI: Institute for Social Research.
Ball-Rokeach, S.
1973   Values and Violence: A Test of the Subculture of Violence Thesis. *American Sociological Review* 38:736–749.
Baskin, Deborah, Sommers, Ira, and Fagan, Jeffrey
1993   The political economy of female violent street crime. *Fordham Urban Law Journal* 20:401–407.
Belenko, Steven A., Fagan, Jeffrey, and Chin, Ko-lin.
1991   Criminal Justice Responses to Crack. *Journal of Research in Crime and Delinquency* 28:55–74.
Bennett, T., and R. Wright
1984   *Burglars on Burglary.* Aldershot, Hants, England: Gower.
Bernard, Thomas
1990   Angry Aggression Among the "Truly Disadvantaged." *Criminology* 28:73–96.
Biernacki, P.
1986   *Pathways from Heroin Addiction: Recovery Without Treatment.* Philadelphia: Temple University Press.

Blom, Maria, and van den Berg, T.
1989   A Typology of the Life and Work Styles of "Heroin-Prostitutes."
        In Maureen Cain (ed.), *Growing Up Good: Policing the Behavior of
        Girls in Europe*. London: Sage.
Blumstein, A., J. Cohen, J. A. Roth, and C. A. Visher (eds.).
1986   *Criminal Careers and Career Criminals*. Washington, DC: National
        Academy Press.
Blumstein, Alfred, David P. Farrington, and Soumyo Moitra.
1985   Delinquency Careers: Innocents, Desisters, and Persisters. In M.
        Tonry and N. Morris (eds.), *Crime and Justice: An Annual Review of
        Research*. Chicago: University of Chicago Press: 187–220.
Bourgois, Phillipe
1989   In search of Horatio Alger: Culture and Ideology in the Crack
        Economy. *Contemporary Drug Problems* 16:619–650.
1995   *In Search of Respect: Selling Crack in El Barrio*. New York: Cam-
        bridge University Press.
Bourgois, Phillipe, and Eloise Dunlap
1993   Exorcising Sex-for-Crack: An Ethnographic Perspective from
        Harlem. In Mitchell S. Ratner (ed.), *Crack Pipe as Pimp: An Ethno-
        graphic Investigation of Sex-for-Crack Exchanges*. New York: Lexing-
        ton Books.
Box, Steven
1987   *Recession, Crime and Punishment*. London: Macmillan.
Brantingham, P., and P. Brantingham
1984   *Patterns in Crime*. New York: Macmillan.
Browne, A.
1987   *When Battered Women Kill*. New York: Free Press.
Bureau of Justice
1996   *Correctional Populations in the United States, 1994*. Washington, DC:
        Department of Justice.
1991   *Women in Prison*. Bureau of Justice Statistics, U.S. Department of
        Justice.
Burkett, Steven, and Eric Jensen
1975   Conventional Ties, Peer Influence, and the Fear of Apprehension:
        A Study of Adolescent Marijuana Use. *Sociological Quarterly*
        16:522–533.
Bursik, Robert J., Jr., and Harold Grasmick
1993   *Neighborhoods and Crime: The Dimensions of Effective Community
        Control*. New York: Lexington Books.
Cameron, Mary Owen
1964   *The Booster and the Snitch*. New York: Free Press.

Campbell, A.
1984   *The Girls in the Gang.* Oxford: Basil Blackwell.
Carlen, P.
1988   *Women, Crime and Poverty.* Milton Keynes: Open University Press.
Caspi, Avshalom, Donald Lyman, Terrie Moffitt, and Phil Silva
n.d.   *Unraveling Girls' Delinquency: Biological, Dispositional, and Contextual Contributions to Adolescent Misbehavior.* Unpublished manuscript.
Cernkovich, Stephen, and P. Giordano
1987   Family relationships and delinquency. *Criminology* 25:295–321.
Chavez, Ernest, Ruth Edwards, and E. R. Oetting
1989   Mexican American and White American School Dropouts' Drug Use, Health Status, and Involvement in Violence. *Public Health Reports* 104:594–604.
Chesney-Lind, M., and R. Shelden
1992   *Girls, Delinquency, and Juvenile Justice.* Pacific Grove, CA: Brooks/Cole.
Chilton, Roland, and S. Datesman
1987   Gender, Race, and Crime: An Analysis of Urban Arrest Trends, 1960–1980. *Gender and Society* 1:152–171.
Chin, K., and J. Fagan
1990   *The Impact of Initiation into Crack on Crime and Drug Use.* Presented at the annual meeting of the American Society of Criminology, Baltimore, November.
Clarke, R., and D. Cornish
1985   Modeling Offenders' Decisions: A Framework for Research and Policy. In M. Tonry and N. Morris (eds.), *Crime and Justice: An Annual Review of Research, Vol. 6.* Chicago: University of Chicago Press: 147–186.
Cocozza, Joseph
1980   *The Effects of Treatment on the Post-Release Experiences of Violent, Mentally Disordered Youths.* New York: N.Y.S. Division of Criminal Justice Services.
Cohen, Bernard
1980   *Deviant Street Networks: Prostitutes in New York.* Lexington, MA: Lexington Books.
Cohen, L., and M. Felson
1979   Social Change and Crime Rate Trends: A Routine Activity Approach. *American Sociological Review* 44:588–608.
Cohen, L., J. Kluegel, and K. Land
1981   Social Inequality and Predatory Criminal Victimization: An Exposition and Test of Formal Theory. *American Sociological Review* 46:505–524.

Colten, Mary Ellen, and Judith E. Marsh
1984　A Sex Roles Perspective on Drug and Alcohol Use by Women. In Cathy Spatz Widom (ed.), *Sex Roles and Psychopathology*. New York: Plenum Press.

Cook, P.
1990　Robbery in the United States: An Analysis of Recent Trends and Patterns. In N. Weiner, M. Zahn, and R. Sagi (eds.), *Violence: Patterns, Causes, Public Policy*. New York: Harcourt Brace Jovanovich: 85–97.
1980　Reducing Injury and Death Rates in Robbery. *Policy Analysis* 6:21–45.
1976　A Strategic Choice Analysis of Robbery. In W. Skogan (ed.), *Sample Surveys of the Victims of Crime*. Cambridge, MA: Ballinger.

Corcoran, Mary, and Susan Parrott
1992　*Black Women's Economic Progress*. Paper presented at the Research Conference on the Urban Underclass: Perspectives from the Social Sciences. Ann Arbor, MI, June.

Cromwell, Paul, James Olson, and D'Aunn Avary
1991　*Breaking and Entering: An Ethnographic Analysis of Burglary*. Newbury Park, CA: Sage.

Curtis, L.
1975　*Violence, Race and Culture*. Lexington, MA: Heath.

Curtis, Richard A., and Lisa Maher
1993　Highly Structured Crack Markets in the Southside of Williamsburg, Brooklyn. In Jeffrey Fagan (ed.), *The Ecology of Crime and Drug Use in Inner Cities*. New York: Social Science Research Council.

Cusson, Maurice, and Pierre Pinsonneault
1986　The Decision to Give Up Crime. In Derek Cornish and Ronald Clarke (eds.), *The Reasoning Criminal: Rational Choice Perspectives on Offending*. New York: Springer-Verlag.

Daily News
1994　The Sick Truth About 140th Street. Brian Kates, p. 12–13.

Daly, K.
1992　Women's Pathways to Felony Court: Feminist Theories of Lawbreaking and Problems of Representation. *Review of Law and Women's Studies* 2:11–52.

Daly, K., and M. Chesney-Lind
1987　Feminism and Criminology. *Justice Quarterly* 5:101–143.

Datesman, Susan, Frank Scarpitti, and Richard Stephenson
1975　Female Delinquency: An Application of Self and Opportunity Theories. *Journal of Research in Crime and Delinquency* 12:107–123.

Deming, Richard
1977   *Women: The New Criminals.* Nashville, TN: Thomas Nelson.
Douthat, S.
1988   Holiday Season Brings the Blues to Incarcerated Mothers. *The Brunswick News*, p. 2.
Duany, J.
1994   *Quisqueya on the Hudson: The Transnational Identity of Dominicans in Washington Heights.* City College of New York, CUNY Dominican Studies Institute.
Dunlap, Eloise
1992   The Impact of Drugs on Family Life and Kin Networks in the Inner-City African-American Single Parent Household. In Adele Harrell and George Peterson (eds.), *Drugs, Crime and Social Isolation: Barriers to Urban Opportunity.* Washington DC: The Urban Institute Press.
Elliott, Delbert, D. Huizinga, and S. Ageton
1985   *Explaining Delinquency and Drug Use.* Beverly Hills, CA: Sage.
Elliott, Delbert, D. Huizinga, and S. Menard
1989   *Multiple Problem Youth: Delinquency, Substance Use and Mental Health Problems.* New York: Springer-Verlag.
Elliott, D., and H. Voss
1974   *Delinquency and Dropout.* Lexington, MA: Lexington Books.
Erickson, Patricia, and Murray, Glenn
1989   Sex differences in Cocaine Use and Experiences: A Double Standard Revived? *American Journal of Drug and Alcohol Abuse* 15:135–152.
Erlanger, H. S.
1974   The Empirical Status of the Subculture of Violence Thesis. *Social Problems* 22:280–292.
Ettore, Elizabeth
1992   *Women and Substance Use.* New Brunswick, NJ: Rutgers University Press.
Fagan, Jeffrey
1994   *Legal and Illegal Work: Crime, Work and Unemployment.* Paper presented at *Metropolitan Assembly on Urban Problems: Linking Research to Action.* Northwestern University, Center for Urban Affairs and Policy Research.
1992   Drug Selling and Licit Income in Distressed Neighborhoods: The Economic Lives of Drug Users and Drug Sellers. In Adele Harrell and George Peterson (eds.), *Drugs, Crime and Social Isolation: Barriers to Urban Opportunity.* Washington DC: The Urban Institute Press.

Fagan, Jeffrey, and Chin, Ko-lin
1990   Violence as Regulation and Social Control in the Distribution of
       Crack. In Mario de la Rosa, Elizabeth Lambert, and Bernard
       Gropper (eds.), *Drugs and Violence*. National Institute on Drug
       Abuse Research Monograph No. 103. DHHS Pub. No.
       (ADM)90–1721. Rockville, MD: U.S. Department of Health and
       Human Services.
1991   Social Processes of Initiation into Crack Use and Dealing. *Journal
       of Drug Issues* 21:313–343.
Fagan, Jeffrey, K. Hansen, and M. Jang
1983   Profiles of Chronically Violent Delinquents: An Empirical Test of
       an Integrated Theory. In J. Kleugel (ed.), *Evaluating Juvenile Jus-
       tice*. Beverly Hills, CA: Sage.
Fagan, J., E. Piper, and Y. T. Cheng
1987   Contributions of Victimization to Delinquency in Inner Cities.
       Journal of Criminal Law and Criminology 78:586–613.
Fagan, J., E. Piper, and M. Moore
1986   Violent Delinquents and Urban Youth. *Criminology* 24:439–472.
Fagan, J., and S. Wexler
1987   Crime in the Home and Crime in the Streets: The Relation Be-
       tween Family Violence and Stranger Crime. *Violence and Victims*
       2:5–21.
Farley, Reynolds
1988   After the Starting Line: Blacks and Women in an Uphill Race. *De-
       mography* 25:447–495.
Farley, Reynolds, and Walter R. Allen
1987   *The Color Line and the Quality of Life in America*. New York: Russell
       Sage Foundation.
Farrington, David
1978   Family Backgrounds of Aggressive Youths. In L. Hersov, M.
       Berger, and D. Shaffer (eds.), *Aggressive and Antisocial Behavior in
       Childhood and Adolescence*. Oxford, England: Pergamon Press.
Faupel, Charles
1991   *Shooting Dope: Career Patterns of Hard-Core Heroin Users*.
       Gainsville: University of Florida Press.
Federal Bureau of Investigation
1993   Uniform Crime Reports, 1992. Washington, DC: U.S. Department
       of Justice.
Feeney, F.
1986   Robbers as Decision-Makers. In D. Cornish and R. Clarke (eds.),
       The Reasoning Criminal: Rational Choice Perspectives on Offending.
       New York: Springer-Verlag: 53–71.

Feinman, Clarice
1986   *Women in the Criminal Justice System*, 2nd ed. New York: Praeger.
Felson, M.
1986   Linking Criminal Choices, Routine Activities, Informal Social Control, and Criminal Outcomes. In D. Cornish and R. Clarke (eds.), *The Reasoning Criminal*. New York: Springer-Verlag: 119–128.
Felson, R.
1993   Predatory and Dispute-Related Violence: A Social Interactionist Approach. In R. Clarke and M. Felson (eds.), *Advances in Criminological Theory, Vol. 5*. Brunswick, NJ: Transaction Press: 103–125.
Felson, M., and L. Cohen
1980   Human Ecology and Crime: A Routine Activity Approach. *Human Ecology* 8:389–406.
Felson, M., and H. Steadman
1983   Situational Factors in Disputes in Leading to Criminal Violence. *Criminology* 21:59–74.
Freedman, M.
1969   *The Process of Work Establishment*. New York: Columbia University Press.
Freeman, Richard
1991   Employment and Earnings of Disadvantaged Young Men in a Labor Shortage Economy. In Christopher Jencks and Paul E. Peterson (eds.), *The Urban Underclass*. Washington DC: The Brookings Institution.
French, John
1993   Pipe Dreams: Crack and the Life in Philadelphia and Newark. In Mitchell S. Ratner (ed.), *Crack Pipe as Pimp: An Ethnographic Investigation of Sex-for-Crack Exchanges*. New York: Lexington Books.
Freud, Sigmund
1933   *New Introductory Lectures on Psychoanalysis*. New York: Norton.
Gabor, T., M. Baril, M. Cusson, D. Elie, M. LeBlanc, and A. Normandeau
1987   *Armed Robber: Cops, Robbers, and Victims*. Springfield, IL: Charles C. Thomas.
Gans, Herbert
1995   *The War Against the Poor, the Underclass and Antipoverty Policy*. New York: Basic Books.
Garbarino, James
1989   The Incidence and Prevalence of Child Maltreatment. In L. Ohlin and M. Tonry (eds.), *Family Violence Crime and Justice: A Review of Research*. Chicago: University of Chicago Press.

Garofalo, J.
1987 Reassessing the Lifestyle Model of Criminal Victimization. In M. Gottfredson and T. Hirschi (eds.), *Positive Criminology*. Newbury Park, CA: Sage.

Gawin, Frank H.
1991 Cocaine Addiction: Psychology and Neurophysiology. *Science* 251:1580–1586.

Geertz, Clifford
1973 *The Interpretation of Cultures*. New York: Basic Books.

Geller, Mark, and L. Ford-Somma
1984 *Violent Homes, Violent Children. A Study of Violence in the Families of Juvenile Offenders*. Division of Juvenile Services, Trenton, NJ: New Jersey State Department of Corrections.

Glick, R., and V. Neto
1977 *National Study of Women's Correctional Programs*. Washington, DC: U.S. Government Printing Office.

Goffman, Erving
1963 *Stigma: Notes on the Management of Spoiled Identity*. Englewood Cliffs, NJ: Prentice-Hall.

Goldstein, Paul J.
1979 *Prostitution and Drugs*. Lexington, MA: Lexington Books.
1985 The Drugs-Violence Nexus: A Tripartite Conceptual Framework. *Journal of Drug Issues* 15:493–506.
1989 Drugs and Violent Crime. In N. A. Weiner and M. E. Wolfgang (eds.), *Pathways to Criminal Violence*. Newbury Park, CA: Sage: 16–48.

Goldstein, Paul J., Henry H. Brownstein, P. Ryan, and P. A. Belluci
1989 Crack and Homicide in New York City, 1989: A Conceptually Based Event Analysis. *Contemporary Drug Problems* 17:109–120.

Goldstein, Paul J., Laurence J. Ouellet, and Michael Fendrich
1992 From Bag Brides to Skeezers: An Historical Perspective on Sex-for-Drugs Behavior. *Journal of Psychoactive Drugs* 24:349–361.

Goldstein, Paul J., Barry Spunt, Patricia Belluci, and Thomas Miller
1991 Volume of Cocaine Use and Violence: A Comparison Between Men and Women. *Journal of Drug Issues* 21:345–367.

Graff, T.
1979 *Personality Characteristics of Battered Women*. Doctoral dissertation, Brigham Young University, Department of Psychology.

Groth, Nicholas
1979 *Men Who Rape: The Psychology of the Offender*. New York: Plenum Press.

Guarino, Susan
1985   *Delinquent Youth and Family Violence: A Study of Abuse and Neglect in the Homes of Serious Juvenile Offenders*. Unpublished manuscript. Boston: Department of Youth Services.

Hagan, John
1994   *Crime and Disrepute*. Thousand Oaks, CA: Pine Forge Press.

Hagan, J., J. H. Simpson, and A. R. Gills
1987   Class in the Household: A Power-Control Theory of Gender and Delinquency. *American Journal of Sociology* 92:788–816.

Hamid, Ansley
1990   The Political Economy of Crack-Related Violence. *Contemporary Drug Problems* 17(1):31–78.
1992   Ethnographic Follow-up of a Predominantly African American Population in a Sample Area in Central Harlem, New York City: Behavioral Causes of the Undercount of the 1990 Census. Washington, DC: Bureau of the Census/Center for Survey Methods Research, U.S. Department of Commerce.

Hanson, Bill, George Beschner, James M. Walters, and Eric Bovelle
1985   *Life with Heroin*. Lexington, MA: Lexington Books.

Harrell, A., and G. Peterson
1992   *Drugs, Crime and Social Isolation*. Washington, DC: The Urban Institute.

Hartnagel, T.
1980   Subculture of Violence: Further Evidence. *Pacific Sociological Review* 23:217–242.

Hartstone, Eliot, and K. Hansen
1984   The Violent Juvenile Offender: An Empirical Portrait. In R. Mathias, P. DeMuro, and R. Allinson (eds.), *An Anthology on Violent Juvenile Offenders*. Newark, NJ: National Council on Crime and Delinquency.

Hayim, G.
1973   Changes in the Criminal Behavior of Heroin Addicts. In *Addiction Research and Treatment Corporation, Interim Report of the First Year of Treatment*. Washington, DC: U.S. Government Printing Office.

Hindelang, Michael
1976   *Criminal Victimization in Eight American Cities*. Cambridge, MA: Ballinger.
1981   Variations in Sex-Race-Age-Specific Incidence Rates of Offending. *American Sociological Review* 46:461–474.

Hirschi, Travis
1969   *Causes of Delinquency*. Berkeley, CA: University of California Press.

Huling, T.
1991   *New York Groups Call on State Lawmakers to Release Women in Prison*. Press Release, The Correctional Association of New York.
Hunt, Dana
1990   Drugs and Consensual Crimes: Drug Dealing and Prostitution. In Michael Tonry and James Q. Wilson (eds.), *Drugs and Crime*. Chicago: University of Chicago Press.
Inciardi, James A., Dorothy Lockwood, and Anne E. Pottieger
1993   *Women and Crack Cocaine*. New York: Macmillan.
Jargowsky, Paul A., and Mary Jo Bane
1990   Ghetto Poverty: Basic Questions. In Lawrence Lynn and Michael G. H. McGeary (eds.), *Inner City Poverty in the United States*. Washington DC: National Academy Press.
1991   Ghetto Poverty in the United States: 1970–80. In Christopher Jencks and Paul E. Peterson (eds.), *The Urban Underclass*. Washington DC: The Brookings Institution.
Jarjoura, G. Roger
1993   Does Dropping out of School Enhance Delinquent Involvement? Results from a Large Scale National Probability Sample. *Criminology* 31:149–172.
Jencks, Christopher
1991   Is the American Underclass Growing? In Christopher Jencks and Paul E. Peterson (eds.), *The Urban Underclass*. Washington DC: The Brookings Institution.
Jensen, G., and D. Brownfield
1986   Gender Lifestyles and Victimization: Beyond Routine Activity Theory. *Violence and Victims* 1:85–89.
Jensen, Gary, and Eve Raymond
1976   Sex Differences in Delinquency. *Criminology* 13:427–448.
Jessor, Richard, and S. Jessor
1977   *Problem Behavior and Psychological Development: A Longitudinal Study of Youth*. New York: Academic Press.
Johnson, Bruce D., Paul J. Goldstein, Edward Preble, James Schmeidler, Douglas Lipton, Barry Spunt, and Thomas Miller
1985   *Taking Care of Business: The Economics of Crime by Heroin Abusers*. Lexington, MA: Lexington Books.
Johnson, Bruce D., Ansley Hamid, and Edmundo Morales
1990   Emerging Models of Crack Distribution. In Thomas Mieczkowski (eds.), *Drugs and Crime: A Reader*. Boston: Allyn and Bacon.
Johnson, Bruce D., Terry Williams, Kojo Dei, and Harry Sanabria
1990   Drug Abuse and the Inner City: Impacts of Hard Drug Use and Sales on Low Income Communities. In James Q. Wilson and

Michael Tonry (eds.), *Drugs and Crime*. Chicago: University of Chicago Press.

Kasarda, John D.
1988   Jobs, Migration and Emerging Urban Mismatches. In Michael G.H. McGeary and Lawrence E. Lynn (eds.), *Urban Change and Poverty*. Washington DC: National Academy Press.
1989   Urban Industrial Transition and the Underclass. *The Annals of the American Academy of Political and Social Science* 501:26–47.

Katz, Jack
1988   *Seductions of Crime: The Sensual and Moral Attractions of Doing Evil*. New York: Basic Books.
1991   The Motivation of the Persistent Robber. In M. Tonry (eds.), *Crime and Justice: A Review of Research, Vol. 14*. Chicago: University of Chicago Press.

Kerr, B.
1985   *Smart Girls, Gifted Women*. Columbus, OH: Ohio Psychology Press.

Kirschenman, J., and K. Neckerman
1991   We'd Love to Hire Them, But . . . : The Meaning of Race for Employers. In C. Jencks and P. Peterson (eds.), *The Urban Underclass*. Washington, DC: The Brookings Institution.

Klemesrud, Judy
1978   Women Terrorists, Sisters in Crime. *New York Times News Service, Honolulu Star Bulletin*, January 16, 1978.

Kornhauser, Ruth
1978   *Social Sources of Delinquency: An Analytic Appraisal of Models*. Chicago: University of Chicago Press.

Krohn, Marvin, and James Massey
1980   Social Control and Delinquent Behavior: An Examination of the Elements of Social Bond. *Sociological Quarterly* 21:529–543.

Kruttschnitt, Candice
1993   Gender and Interpersonal Violence. In A. Reiss and J. Roth (eds.), *Understanding and Preventing Violence, Vol. 3*. National Academy of Science. Panel on the Understanding and Control of Violent Behavior, Washington, DC.

LaGrange, Randy, and Helene Raskin White
1985   Age Differences in Delinquency: A Test of Theory. *Criminology* 23:19–45.

Lake, Elise
1993   An Exploration of the Violent Victim Experiences of Female Offenders. *Violence and Victims* 8:41–51.

Lane, Roger
1986   *Roots of Violence in Black Philadelphia, 1860–1900*. Cambridge, MA:
        Harvard University Press.
Laub, John, and R. Sampson
1993   Turning Points in the Life Course: Why Change Matters to the
        Study of Crime. *Criminology* 31:301–326.
Lauritsen, J., R. Sampson, and J. Laub
1991   The Link Between Offending and Victimization Among Adoles-
        cents. *Criminology* 29:265–292.
Le Blanc, M., and M. Frechette
1989   *Male Criminal Activity from Childhood Through Youth*. New York:
        Springer-Verlag.
Lejeune, R.
1977   The Management of a Mugging. *Urban Life* 6:123–148.
Leonard, Eileen
1982   *Women, Crime and Society: A Critique of Criminology*. New York:
        Longman.
Lewis, Dorothy, S. Shanok, J. Pincus, and G. Glaser
1979   Violent Juvenile Delinquents: Psychiatric, Neurological, Psycho-
        logical and Abuse Factors. *Journal of the American Academy of Child
        Psychiatry* 18:307–319.
Liebow, Elliot
1967   Tally's Corner: A Study of Negro Streetcorner Men. Boston: Little,
        Brown.
Loeber, Rolf, and M. Stoudthamer-Loeber
1986   Models and Meta-Analyses of the Relationship Between Family
        Variables and Juvenile Conduct Problems and Delinquency. In N.
        Morris and M. Tonty (eds.), *Crime and Justice: An Annual Review of
        Research, Vol. 7*. Chicago: University of Chicago Press.
Loeber, Rolf, and P. Wikstrom
1993   Individual Pathways to Crime in Different Types of Neighbor-
        hoods. In D. Farrington (ed.), *Integrating Individual and Ecological
        Aspects of Crime*. Stockholm, Sweden: The National Council for
        Crime Prevention.
Loftin, Colin, and Robert Hill
1974   Regional Subculture and Homicide: An Examination of the
        Gastil-Hackney Thesis. *American Sociological Review* 39:714–724.
Lombroso, Cesare, and William Ferrero
1895   *The Female Offender*. London: Fisher Unwin.
Los Angeles Times
1996   *As Bad as They Want to Be*. Elizabeth Mehren, E1–3.

Luckenbill, D.
1980   Patterns of Force in Robbery. *Deviant Behavior* 1:361–378.
MacCoun, Robert, and Peter Reuter
1992   Are the Wages of Sin $30 an Hour? Economic Aspects of Street-Level Drug Dealing. *Crime and Delinquency* 38:477–491.
Maher, Lisa, and Richard Curtis
1993   Women on the Edge of Crime: Crack Cocaine and the Changing Contexts of Street Level Sex Work in New York City. *Crime, Law and Social Change* 18:221–258.
Mann, C. R.
1988   Getting Even? Women Who Kill in Domestic Encounters. *Justice Quarterly* 5:33–51.
Mare, Robert D., and Christopher Winship
1991   Socioeconomic Change and the Decline of Marriage for Blacks and Whites. In Christopher Jencks and Paul E. Peterson (eds.), *The Urban Underclass*. Washington DC: The Brookings Institution.
Massey, Douglas S., and Mitchell L. Eggers
1990   The Ecology of Inequality: Minorities and the Concentration of Poverty, 1970–80. *American Journal of Sociology* 95:1153–1188.
Matsueda, Ross, and K. Heimer
1987   Race, Family Structure, and Delinquency: A Test of Differential Association and Social Control Theories. *American Sociological Review* 52:826–840.
McCord, Joan
1979   A Thirty Year Follow-up of Treatment Effects. *American Psychologist* 33:284–289.
Megargee, E.
1982   Psychological Determinants and Correlates of Criminal Violence. In M. E. Olfgang and N. A. Weiner (eds.), *Criminal Violence*. Beverly Hills, CA: Sage.
Meisenhelder, Thomas
1977   An Exploratory Study of Exiting From Criminal Careers. *Criminology* 15:319–334.
Merton, Robert
1957   *Social Theory and Social Structure*. Glencoe, IL: Free Press.
Messner, Steven
1983   Regional and Racial Effects on the Urban Homicide Rate: The Subculture of Violence Revisited. *American Journal of Sociology* 88:997–1007.
Miller, Eleanor
1986   *Street Woman*. Philadelphia: Temple University Press.

Moore, Joan
1993   *Going Down to the Barrio: Homeboys and Homegirls in Change.*
        Philadelphia: Temple University Press.
Morris, Ruth
1964   Female Delinquency and Relational Problems. *Social Forces*
        43:82–88.
Moss, Phillip, and Christopher Tilly
1991   *Why Black Men Are Doing Worse in the Labor Market: A Review of*
        Supply-Side and Demand-Side Explanations. Paper prepared for the
        Social Science Research Council, Committee on Research on the
        Urban Underclass, Subcommittee on Joblessness and the Under-
        class. New York: Social Science Research Council.
Moss, S.
1986   Women in Prison: A Case of Pervasive Neglect. *Women and Ther-*
        apy 5:5.
Mulvey, Edward P., and Mark Aber
1988   Growing Out of Delinquency: Development and Desistance. In
        Richard L. Jenkins and Waln K. Brown (eds.), *The Abandonment of*
        Delinquent Behavior: Promoting the Turnaround. New York: Praeger:
        99–116.
Murphy, Sheila, Dan Waldorf, and Craig Reinarman
1991   Drifting into Dealing: Becoming a Cocaine Seller. *Qualitative Soci-*
        ology 13:321–343.
Myers, M.
1989   Symbolic Policy and the Sentencing of Drug Offenders. *Law and*
        Society Review 23:295–315.
Naffine, Ngaire
1987   *Female Crime: The Construction of Women in Criminology.* Sydney,
        Australia: Allen and Unwin.
Newsweek
1992   *It's Not Just New York . . .* March 9: 25–27.
New York City Department of City Planning
1991   *Annual Report on Social Indicators.* New York: Department of City
        Planning.
1992   *Annual Report on Social Indicators.* New York: Department of City
        Planning.
New York Times
1989a   Report from the Field on an Endless War. March 12, Section IV, p.
        5.
1989b   Selling Milk, Bread, and Cocaine in New York. March 30, B1.
1990   As Bad as They Want to Be. Elizabeth Mehren, B1–B4.

1993   Ex-inmates Urge Return to Areas of Crime to Help. Francis Clines, B1–B3.

1994   Three Decades in Free Fall: The Sad Saga of 140th Street. Douglas Martin, B6.

1995   Two Women Charged in Series of Brooklyn Armed Robberies. Garry Pierre-Pierre, B1–B3.

Noblit, George, and Janie Burcart

1976   Women and Crime: 1960–1970. *Social Science Quarterly* 56:650–657.

Nurco, D., and R. Dupont

1977   A Preliminary Report of Crime and Addiction Within a Community-Wide Population of Narcotics Addicts. *Drug and Alcohol Dependence* 2:109–121.

Oliver, Melvin

1995   Commentary. In M. Belinda Tucker and C. Michell-Kernan (eds.), *The Decline in Marriage Among African Americans*. New York: Russell Sage Foundation.

Osgood, Wayne, L. Johnston, P. O'Malley, and J. Bachman

1988   The Generality of Deviance in Late Adolescence and Early Adulthood. *American Sociological Review* 53:81–93.

Osterman, P.

1980   *Getting Started: The Youth Labor Market*. Cambridge, MA: MIT Press.

Ouellet, Lawrence J., W. Wayne Wiebel, A. D. Jimenez, and W. A. Johnson

1993   Crack Cocaine and the Transformation of Prostitution in Three Chicago Neighborhoods. In Mitchell S. Ratner (ed.), *Crack Pipe as Pimp: An Ethnographic Investigation of Sex-for-Crack Exchanges*. New York: Lexington Books.

Owens, David and M. Straus

1975   The Social Structure of Violence in Childhood and Approval of Violence as an Adult. *Aggressive Behavior* 1:193–211.

Padilla, Felix

1992   *The Gang as an American Enterprise*. Boston, MA: Northeastern University Press.

Park Slope Paper

1989   Women Robbers Apprehended. August 25, p. 1.

Parker, Robert Nash

1989   Poverty, Subculture of Violence, and Type of Homicide. *Social Forces* 67:983–1007.

Patterson, Gerald

1984   Siblings: Fellow Travelers in Coercive Family Process. In Robert Blanchard and D. Caroline Blanchard (eds.), *Advances in the Study of Aggression, Vol. 1*. Orlando, FL: Academic Press.

Patterson, Gerald, and T. Dishion
1985   Contributions of Families and Peers to Delinquency. *Criminology* 23:63–80.

Peters, Jan
1993   Hip Hop's New Hardcore Females. *Word Up*, May:14–16.

Petersilia, J., P. Greenwood, and M. Lavin
1977   *Criminal Careers of Habitual Felons.* Santa Monica, CA: RAND.

Pettiway, Leon
1987   Participation in Crime Partnerships by Female Drug Users: The Effects of Domestic Arrangements, Drug Use, and Criminal Involvement. *Criminology* 25:741–766.

Pickles, Andrew, and Michael Rutter
1991   Statistical and Conceptual Models of "Turning Points" in Developmental Processes. In D. Magnusson, L. Bergman, G. Rudinger, and B. Torestad (eds.), *Problems and Methods in Longitudinal Research: Stability and Change.* New York: Cambridge University Press: 110–136.

Pipher, Mary
1994   *Reviving Ophelia: Saving the Selves of Adolescent Girls.* New York: Ballantine Books.

Pollack-Byrne, J.
1990   *Women, Prison and Crime.* Belmont, CA: Brooks/Cole.

Pollak, Otto
1950   *The Criminality of Women.* Philadelphia: University of Pennsylvania Press.

Potts, D., S. Herzberger, and A. Holland
1979   *Child Abuse: A Cross-Generational Pattern of Child Rearing.* Paper presented at the Midwestern Psychological Association Convention, Chicago, May.

Price, B., and N. Sokoloff
1982   *The Criminal Justice System and Women.* New York: Clark Boardman.

Rankin, Joseph
1980   School Factors and Delinquency: Interactions by Age and Sex. *Social Science Research* 64:420–434.

Ratner, Mitchell
1993   Sex, Drugs, and Public Policy: Studying and Understanding the Sex-for-Crack Phenomenon. In Mitchell S. Ratner (ed.), *Crack Pipe as Pimp: An Ethnographic Investigation of Sex-for-Crack Exchanges.* New York: Lexington Books.

Ray, Marsh
1961   The Cycle of Abstinence and Relapse Among Heroin Addicts. *Social Problems* 9:132–140.

Reinarman, Craig, Dan Waldorf, and Sheila Murphy
1989   *The Call of the Pipe: Freebasing and Crack Use as Norm-Bound Episodic Compulsion.* Paper presented at the annual meeting of the American Society of Criminology, Reno, NV, November.

Rengert, G., and J. Wasilchick
1985   *Suburban Burglary: A Time and a Place for Everything.* Springfield, IL: Charles C. Thomas.

Reuter, Peter, Robert MacCoun, and Patrick Murphy
1990   *Money from Crime.* Report R–3894. Santa Monica, CA: Rand Corporation.

Ricketts, Errol, and Isabel Sawhill
1988   Defining and Measuring the Underclass. *Journal of Policy Analysis and Management* 7:316–325.

Robbins, Lee, W. Bates, and P. O'Neal
1962   Adult Drinking Patterns of Former Problem Children. In D. Pittman and C. Snyder (eds.), *Society, Culture and Drinking Practices.* New York: Wiley.

Roman, L.
1990   Jailed Mothers Risk Losing Their Kids. *New Directions for Women,* March/April: 12.

Rosenbaum, Marsha
1981   *Women and Heroin.* New Brunswick, NJ: Rutgers University Press.

Ross, Richard, and Marjorie Cohen
1988   *New York State Trends in Felony Drug Processing, 1983–1987.* Albany: New York Division of Criminal Justice Services.

Rowe, David, and Bill Gulley
1992   Sibling Effects on Substance Use and Delinquency. *Criminology* 30:217–223.

Sampson, Robert J.
1985   Race and Criminal Violence: A Demographically Disaggregated Analysis of Urban Homicide. *Crime and Delinquency* 31:47–82.
1986   Effects of Socioeconomic Context on Official Reaction to Juvenile Delinquency. *American Sociological Review* 51:876–885.
1987   Urban Black Violence: The Effect of Male Joblessness and Family Disruption. *American Journal of Sociology* 93:348–382.
1992   Family Management and Child Development: Insights from Social Disorganization Theory. In Joan McCord (ed.), *Facts, Forecasts, and Frameworks.* New Brunswick, NJ: Transaction Publishers: 63–92.

Sampson, R., and W. B. Groves
1989   Community Structure and Crime: Testing Social-Disorganization Theory. *American Journal of Sociology* 94:774–802.

Sampson, R., and J. Lauritsen
1994   Individual and Community Factors in Violent Offending and Victimization. In A. J. Reiss, Jr., and J. A. Roth (eds.), *Understanding and Controlling Violence, Vol. 3.* Washington, DC: National Academy Press: 1–114.
1990   Deviant Lifestyles, Proximity to Crime, and the Offender-Victim Link in Personal Violence. *Journal of Research on Crime and Delinquency* 27:110–139.
Sarri, R.
1987   Unequal Protection Under the Law: Women and the Criminal Justice System. In J. Figueira-McDonough and R. Sarri (eds.), *The Trapped Woman: Catch-22 in Deviance and Control.* Newbury Park, CA: Sage: 394–427.
Sassen-Koob, Sassia
1989   New York City's Informal Economy. In Alejandro Portes, Manuel Castells, and Lauren A. Benton (eds.), *The Informal Economy: Studies in Advanced and Less Developed Countries.* Baltimore: Johns Hopkins University Press.
Schur, E.
1971   *Labeling Deviant Behavior: Its Sociological Implications.* New York: Harper and Row.
Shaw, C.
1966   *The Jack-Roller.* Chicago: University of Chicago Press.
Shover, Neil
1983   The Latter Stages of Ordinary Property Offenders' Careers. *Social Problems* 31:208–218.
1985   *Aging Criminals.* Newbury Park, CA: Sage.
Shover, Neil, and Carol Thompson
1992   Age, Differential Expectations, and Crime Desistance. *Criminology* 30:89–104.
Siegel, Ronald K.
1987   Cocaine Smoking: Nature and Extent of Coca Paste and Cocaine Freebase Abuse. In Arnold M. Washton and Mark Gold (eds.), *Cocaine: A Clinician's Handbook.* New York: Guilford Press.
Simcha-Fagan, Ora, and M. Silver
1982   *Social Background, Parental Predisposition, and Delinquent Behavior: An Examination of the Effect of Family Socialization.* Paper presented at the annual meeting of the American Society of Criminology.
Simon, Rita James
1975   *Women and Crime.* Lexington, MA: D. C. Heath.

Simons, R. L., M. G. Miller, and S. M. Aigner
1980   Contemporary Theories of Deviance and Female Delinquency: An Empirical Test. *Journal of Research in Crime and Delinquency* 17:42.

Skogan, Wesley
1990   *Disorder and Decline: Crime and the Spiral of Decay in American Neighborhoods.* New York: Free Press.

Smith, Douglas
1979   Sex and Deviance: An Assessment of Major Sociological Variables. *Sociological Quarterly* 20:183.

Smith, Douglas, and Raymond Paternoster
1987   The Gender Gap in Theories of Deviance: Issues and Evidence. *Journal of Research in Crime and Delinquency* 24:140–172.

Sommers, I., and D. Baskin
1992   Sex, Race, Age and Violent Offending. *Violence and Victims* 7:191–202.
1993   The Situational Context of Violent Female Offending. *Journal of Research in Crime and Delinquency* 30:136–162.

Sommers, I., D. Baskin, and J. Fagan
1996   The Structural Relationship Between Drug Use, Drug Dealing and Other Income Support Activities Among Women Drug Dealers. *Journal of Drug Issues* 26:975–1006.

Sorrells, James
1977   Kids Who Kill. *Crime and Delinquency* 23:312–320.

Sowder, B., and M. R. Burt
1980   *Children of Heroin Addicts: An Assessment of Health, Learning, Behavioral, and Adjustment Problems.* New York: Praeger.

Spitz, Harry, and Rosecan, Jeffrey
1987   Cocaine Reconceptualized: Historical Overview. In Henry I. Spitz and Jeffrey S. Rosecan (eds.), *Cocaine Abuse: New Directions in Treatment and Research.* New York: Brunner/Mazel.

Stall, Ron, and Patrick Biernacki
1986   Spontaneous Remission from the Problematic Use of Substances: An Inductive Model Derived from a Comparative Analysis of the Alcohol, Opiate, Tobacco, and Food/Obesity Literatures. *International Journal of the Addictions* 2:1–23.

Stattin, H., and D. Magnusson
1990   *Pubertal Maturation in Female Development.* Hillsdale, NJ: Erlbaum.

Steffensmeier, D.
1983   Organization Properties and Sex-Segregation in the Underworld: Building a Sociological Theory of Sex Differences in Crime. *Social Forces* 61:1010–1032.

Steffensmeier, D., and Allan, E. A.
1988   Sex Disparities in Arrests by Residence, Race and Age: An Assessment of the Gender Convergence/Crime Hypothesis. *Justice Quarterly* 5:53–80.

Steffensmeier, D., and C. Steifel
1992   Time-Series Analysis of the Female Percentage of Arrests for Property Crimes, 1960–1985: A Test of Alternative Explanation. *Justice Quarterly* 9:77–104.

Stephens, Richard C.
1991   *The Street Addict Role: A Theory of Heroin Addiction.* Albany, NY: State University of New York Press.

Straus, Murray, R. Gelles, and S. Steinmetz
1980   *Behind Closed Doors: Violence in the American Family.* New York: Doubleday.

Sullivan, Mercer
1989   *Getting Paid.* Ithaca, NY: Cornell University Press.

Sutherland, Edwin
1939   *Principles of Criminology*, 3rd ed. Philadelphia: Lippincott.

Sykes, Gresham, and David Matza
1957   Techniques of Neutralization: A Theory of Delinquency. *American Journal of Sociology*, 22:664–670.

Thomas, P.
1974   *Down These Mean Streets.* New York: Vintage Press.

Thornberry, T., M. Moore, and R. L. Christenson
1985   The Effect of Dropping Out of High School on Subsequent Criminal Behavior. *Criminology* 23:3–18.

Tienda, Marta
1989   *Neighborhood Effects and the Formation of the Underclass.* Paper presented at the annual meeting of the American Sociological Association, San Francisco, August.

Tittle, Charles, M. J. Burke, and E. Jackson
1986   Modeling Sutherland's Theory of Differential Association: Toward an Empirical Classification. *Social Forces* 65:405–432.

Tobier, Emanuel
1984   *The Changing Face of Poverty: Trends in New York City's Population in Poverty, 1960–1990.* New York: Community Service Society.

Travisano, R.
1970   Alteration and Conversion as Qualitatively Different Transformations. In G. Stone and H. Farberman (eds.), *Social Psychology Through Symbolic Interaction.* Cambridge: MA: Ginn-Blaisdell: 594–605.

Tucker, M. B., and C. Mitchell-Kernan
1995   *The Decline in Marriage Among African Americans.* New York: Russell Sage Foundation.

Valentine, Bettylou
1978   *Hustling and Other Hard Work: Life Styles in the Ghetto.* New York: Free Press.

Voss, H., and R. Stephens
1973   Criminality History of Narcotic Addicts. *Drug Forum* 2:191–202.

Wacquant, Loic D., and William J. Wilson
1989   The Costs of Racial and Class Exclusion in the Inner City. *Annals of the American Academy of Political and Social Science* 501:8–25.

Waldorf, Dan, Craig Reinarman, and Sheila Murphy
1991   *Cocaine Changes: The Experiences of Using and Quitting.* Philadelphia: Temple University Press.

Walsh, D.
1986   *Heavy Business: Commercial Burglary and Robbery.* London: Routledge and Kegan Paul.
1980   *Break-Ins: Burglary from Private Houses.* London: Constable.

Warr, Mark, and M. Stafford
1991   The Influence of Delinquent Peers: What They Think or What They Do? *Criminology* 29:851–866.

Weiner, N., and M. Wolfgang
1989   *Pathways to Criminal Violence.* Newbury Park, CA: Sage.

Weisheit, R., and S. Mahan
1988   *Women, Crime and Criminal Justice.* Cincinnati, OH: Anderson Publishing.

Weismann, J. C., P. L. Katsampes, and T. G. Giacinti
1976   Opiate Use and Criminality Among a Jail Population. *Addictive Diseases* 1:269–281.

White, Helene R.
1992   Early Problem Behavior and Later Drug Problems. *Journal of Research in Crime and Delinquency* 29:412–429.

Williams, K.
1984   Economic Sources of Homicide: Reestimating the Effects of Poverty and Inequality. *American Sociological Review* 49:283–289.

Williams, Kirk, and R. Flewelling
1987   The Social Production of Criminal Homicide: A Comparative Study of Disaggregated Rates in American Cities. *American Sociological Review* 53:421–431.

Williams, Terry
1989   *Cocaine Kids.* Reading, MA: Addison-Wesley.
1992   *Crackhouse.* Reading, MA: Addison-Wesley.

Wilson, James Q., and Richard Hernstein
1985   *Crime and Human Nature.* New York: Simon and Schuster.
Wilson, William J.
1987   *The Truly Disadvantaged.* Chicago: University of Chicago Press.
1991   Studying Inner-City Social Dislocations: The Challenge of Public
         Agenda Research. *American Sociological Review* 56:1–14.
1996   *When Work Disappears: The World of the New Urban Poor.* New
         York: Knopf.
Wolfgang, M. E.
1958   *Patterns in Criminal Homicide.* Montclair, NJ: Patterson Smith.
Wolfgang, M. E., and Ferracuti, F.
1975   *The Subculture of Violence: Toward an Integrated Theory in Criminol-*
         ogy. London: Tavistock.
Young, Randy
1978   Dodge City, The Deadliest Precinct in Town. *New York,* August 28:
         43–45.
Zimmer, L.
1987   *Operation Pressure Point.* An Occasional Paper of the Center for
         Crime and Justice, New York University School of Law.
Zucker, Robert
1991   The Concept of Risk and the Etiology of Alcoholism: A Proba-
         bilistic-Developmental Perspective. In D. Pittman and H. R.
         White (eds.), *Society, Culture and Drinking Patterns Reexamined.*
         New Brunswick, NJ: Rutgers Center of Alcohol Studies: 513–532.

Index

Adler, Freda, 5
Adler, Patricia, 96, 113, 125, 139, 142
Adolescence
   and peers, 64, 68–70
   problem behavior syndrome, 70, 75
   See also Initiation into criminality
Age
   and arrest data, 21–24, 88
   and desistance, 139, 140–141
   and male criminality, 22
   See also Adolescence; Initiation into
     criminality
Agnew, Robert, 68
Aigner, S. M., 5
Akers, Ronald, 68
Alcohol abuse, 54, 57. *See also* Drug
   abuse
Alexander, Priscilla, 4
Alfaro, Jose, 54
Allan, E.A., 20
Allen, Walter R., 29
Althaus, 96
Anderson, Elijah, 35, 40, 53, 54, 56,
   60–61, 63, 64, 66, 82, 96, 117, 118
Anderson, Linda, 5
Arnold, R., 2, 69
Arrest data, 8, 11–12, 19
   and age, 21–24, 88
   arrest rates, 20–21
   drug-related, 33–34
   and patterns of criminality, 13
   and sex-race-age groups, 20–24
Assault, 15
   arrest rates, 22–24
   and crack-cocaine industry, 120–123
   dispute-related, 116
   and domestic violence, 114

   as face-saving behavior, 117
   motivation for, 111
   percent of interviewees involved in,
     126(n1)
   planning and decisions, 118–119, 124
   and rational planning, 124
   and respect, 117–118
   and retaliation, 117
   situational characteristics, 114
   stages, 115–116
   third parties, 116–117
   and verbal conflict, 115–116
   and victim aggression, 116–117, 123
   See also Robbery
Austin, Roy, 5
Awareness space, 111–112

Bachman, Jerald, 63
Ball-Rokeach, S., 25
Bane, Mary Jo, 27, 29, 78(n1)
Baron, 71
Baskin, Deborah R., 32, 98, 120
Bayview Correctional Facility, 11
Bedford Hills Correctional Facility, 11,
   133
Belenko, Steven A., 33, 149
Biernacki, Patrick, 124, 137, 141, 142
Black women
   arrest rates, 21, 24, 26
   and crack-cocaine industry, 56
   and poverty, 27–28
Blom, Maria, 98, 113
Blumstein, A., 33, 143(n1)
Bounded spheres of interaction, 6
Bourgois, Phillipe, 31, 40, 81, 82, 96, 99,
   151(n1)
Box, Steven, 6